INVISIBLE
BATTLEGROUNDS

INVISIBLE BATTLEGROUNDS

Winning the War
in the Body, Mind,
& Spiritual Realm

Yolanda Stith

DESTINY IMAGE® PUBLISHERS, INC.
PO Box 310, Shippensburg, PA 17257-0310
"Promoting Inspired Lives."

This book and all other Destiny Image and Destiny Image Fiction books are available at Christian bookstores and distributors worldwide.

Cover design by Eileen Rockwell
Interior design by Terry Clifton

For more information on foreign distributors, call 717-532-3040.
Or reach us on the Internet: www.destinyimage.com

ISBN 13 TP: 978-0-7684-4651-7
ISBN 13 EBook: 978-0-7684-4652-4
HC ISBN: 978-0-7684-4654-8
LP ISBN:978-0-7684-4653-1

For Worldwide Distribution, Printed in the U.S.A.
1 2 3 4 5 6 / 22 21 20 19

Acknowledgments

I'D LIKE TO THANK EVERYONE FOR YOUR PRAYERS FOR me while I worked on this project. You're amazing!

Special thanks to:

The precious Holy Spirit, you have always been a constant friend and comforter. Through every season of my life, You have NEVER failed.

Kori Stith Sr., my amazing husband, who told me not to quit every single time I said I would.

Drs. Matthew and Kamilah Stevenson, for believing that I could do and be all that God has created me to be!

Apostle John Eckhardt, for the writers impartation, it accelerated me further into my purpose.

Kimberly J. Martin, you are my wonderful blessing.

CONTENTS

FOREWORD

I WANT TO PERSONALLY ENDORSE AND RECOMMEND THIS book by Yolanda Stith. I believe the insight and revelation you will receive in this book will be major tools for your life. Yolanda has unraveled truths concerning the invisible battleground through her life experiences and the Word of God. Her insight concerning this subject is full of wisdom and power

Invisible Battlegrounds will assist you and properly equip you to fight the powers of darkness. The realm of the invisible battleground is difficult for many to understand. I have taught on the reality of spiritual warfare for many years, and it takes wisdom from God to comprehend the importance of this subject.

The truths in this book will help you walk in victory. The invisible realm determines what occurs in the physical realm. Because it is not seen by the natural eye, it is usually hidden from view. It takes discernment and revelation to comprehend this realm. This is why the truths in this book are important for you as a believer. These truths will help you navigate the spiritual realm that determines the physical realm.

What Yolanda has learned through experience will help you win the battles that you encounter. There is a wealth of information in this book that will contribute to the growing knowledge of spiritual warfare. We cannot be ignorant of Satan's devices. Ignorance is a sure way to suffer defeat. Knowledge and wisdom are essential to win this battle.

As you read the words in this book, I pray the Lord will give you understanding in a subject that is often difficult to comprehend. Many believers draw back from this subject because of its difficulty. Do not be afraid to study and grow in knowledge in this area. This book will assist you in your growth and development as a believer.

Yolanda Stith has a proven ministry. I have seen her work and faithfulness over the years. Her success can be traced to her willingness to fight and teach on this subject. I want you to hear the words of her heart that are expressed in this new release.

JOHN ECKHARDT
Bestselling author of *Prayers That Rout Demons*

INTRODUCTION

B<small>Y THE TIME</small> I <small>WAS NINETEEN YEARS OLD,</small> I <small>HAD</small> already suffered two nervous breakdowns and by then, I'd been battling depression all of my life. Although I didn't know then what I know now, I could look at the lives of almost everyone in my family, particularly the women, and see that there was something that hovered over us—gripped us—and left each of us weakened and defeated.

I now understand that I was not battling mental illness, but a generational curse that was one of the powerful forces sent by hell to push me to the edge of my sanity and ultimately leave me there clinging to what little hope I had left.

And then, one day, Jesus reeled me back in, back to life, and back to Himself. That was the day I decided that I wanted to know more about God. I turned my life over to Him, fully and completely. The reality that He had power over life and death struck me in a real way. I wanted Him. I *needed* Him. I wanted to make Him Lord, and He was right there, waiting with open arms. Right there, in the midst of my despair, God reminded me that He never abandoned me. He and I had been in this place before.

I vividly remember the very moment I was called to follow Jesus. I was nine years of age and, if I close my eyes right now, the vision that I had that night would come right back me. There I was, this little girl, standing in the center of a huge room literally surrounded by people. They were everywhere! Some faces were familiar to me, others not so much. While everyone in the room seemed to be oblivious to me, my eyes darted from one person to the next, attempting to make sense of where I was and why we were gathered together in this big house.

But before I could process what was happening around me, in a flash, the house begins to fill with water right before my eyes. Within what felt like a matter of seconds, the entire room flooded and the people were flapping their arms and gasping for air as they were being swept away by the waves. Everyone was literally drowning—everyone but me.

The water eventually covered my head as I looked toward the ceiling. The sun was shining so brightly through the water, and then it happened. I heard a loud, clear voice. It was the voice of the Father. He said, "As quickly as this room has filled with water is as quickly as My Son will return."

Then I woke up. At nine years of age, I had no idea what I'd just experienced. I hadn't attended any church services, I wasn't saved and neither was anyone in my house. I heard some adults speak about God and the Bible, but I had never been formally introduced to Him. Still, there was something so familiar and safe about His voice and His presence, even in my dreams. It was then that I dedicated my life to following God; and from that day forward, I never forgot.

God knew that nine-year-old little girl needed Him. He knew that nineteen-year-old young woman needed Him. He certainly knew that this apostolic woman with a destiny to carry His name and His word across oceans, nations, and continents would need Him—every day, every moment, and every breath of her life. I knew it too.

That encounter left a permanent impression on my heart and soul. I was marked and life's circumstances couldn't change that. Premarital sex that would eventually lead to pregnancy outside of wedlock couldn't change that. All of the anger and bitterness I battled couldn't change that. Depression couldn't change that. When He pulled me from the edge of that emotional cliff that day, I decided who I was, who I am. I am a child of God, and so are you!

You are called to rise! You, man of God, you, woman of God, have been called to blaze trails. You have been called to move mountains. You are emerging; and if you are holding this book in your hands, I believe it is because you know that there is indeed a call from God on your life.

However, you may be in a place where you feel disconnected from that call. You may feel misunderstood, fearful, abused, and done with church as a whole. You may feel marred and that God is unable to use you. Well, you have come to right place. You were created and chosen by God to soar like an eagle.

This book will give you the courage and the tools you need to spread your wings and to do what has never been done before—to show the world how bold and brave His sons and daughters can be. Nations mourn because fear has kept Kingdom men and women from taking their rightful place for far too long. There's a whole world waiting for *you* to take your place. It's time for you to *rise!* Let's discover how.

CHAPTER 1

INVISIBLE BATTLEGROUNDS DEFINED

I REMEMBER BEING SIX YEARS OF AGE AND USHERED INTO an external and internal war zone without the proper tools needed to skillfully navigate through its constant twists and turns. By that time, my mother had suffered an extremely traumatic accident causing severe and permanent brain damage and my father was an alcoholic who could not properly care for, my sister and I.

Although it was quite unclear to me and I couldn't understand it at the time, I can now look back in reflection and properly articulate the outline and complete structure of hell's assignment against my life and the invisible battleground I was standing directly in the center of and didn't have a clue! Because I didn't have a spiritual foundation or insight, it was impossible for me to engage in warfare and dismantle the enemy seeking to destroy me.

When you think of a battleground, it's quite normal to imagine soldiers in combat. On opposite sides of a field are enemies at war against one another, both vigorously pursuing the same goal—victory. In war, the battlegrounds (also known as combat zones), are marked territories set aside for strictly that purpose, war. When it's time for matters to be settled, both sides would gather and head to the battlegrounds to "duke it out" and fairly determine who will walk away with the winning title. One thing you'll notice is that everyone involved in these types of battles are of age and have personally consented.

Another example of a battleground is found on our map. In the United States, we have what are called "battleground states," also known as "swing states." What this means is that during elections and competitive rallies, the two major political parties have a strong and fair shot at claiming the winner's seat because they each have like amounts of support among the people. Again, those who are able to participate in the electoral process are those who are of age and have been given permission to cast their vote for whichever side they stand on.

The reason this is relevant enough to point out is because it highlights just how strong both sides coming to battle are. What it also shows us is just how divided the people are. Now, not all states are battleground states, so in many places during political rallies, one side has the upper hand by a landslide and the other doesn't have a shot at winning at all. In those types of matches, it's usually quite clear from the beginning who will win in the end. This is mostly because the people are more unified in their beliefs and there are more for them than there are those against them. Sometimes, it all comes down to who you have on your team and standing in your corner. Ecclesiastes 9:11 (KJV) says:

> *I returned, and saw under the sun, that the race is not to the swift, nor the battle to the strong, neither yet bread to the wise, nor yet riches to men of understanding, nor yet favour to men of skill; but time and chance happeneth to them all.*

This Scripture is befitting for both the natural and the spiritual. See, the length of a battle is not always easily predictable. Some can be pretty short, while others, well, others can last for quite some time. In the scenarios given, I want you to picture that each team starts out fully equipped, fully staffed, and ready for battle. Somewhere between the beginning and the middle of the battle though, you'll imagine that there are fewer and fewer soldiers on the battleground. Some, falling victim to their opponent amid the battle, draw their last breath, having their remains removed from the grounds. And then there are the others who willfully relinquish their "active-duty" status and give up as they decidedly bow to their (temporary) physical state and walk off of the battleground—*while their cohorts are still fighting.*

By the end of the battle, the number of soldiers left do not at all mirror the amount when both sides started; and well, the few who remain are determined—they're going to fight to the finish. In the natural and in the spirit, the battle is always won by those who remain in the fight until the end!

Much like these natural, visible battlegrounds, the invisible battlegrounds I want to unfold in the upcoming pages are those designated areas in our lives where battles take place—in our minds, our flesh, and in our spirits. There are spiritual forces at work above us, around us, beneath us, and *within* us at all times. It's important that we not only understand these forces, but that we also determine which side we're on so that we can suit up and fight back!

In order to fight back, we need to be armed with the proper equipment that will ensure that the victory is ours. See, the thing about warring in the spirit is that *we have help!* Christ Himself is standing in our corner! With Christ on our team, losing is not our portion. Romans 8:31 says, *"What, then, shall we say in response to these things? If God is for us, who can be against us?"* That alone tells us that it doesn't matter how large our opponent is or how outnumbered we may be; First Corinthians 15:57 says, *"But thanks be to God! He gives us the victory through our Lord Jesus Christ."* We won from the beginning! Jesus secured the victory and handed it to us upon His death on the cross.

The reason I found it important enough to point out the fact that in both examples given, in each scenario, all participants are of age, is because it's important to note that hell does not always play fair. Satan launches attacks against children primarily because of their inability to fight back and because he is aware of their future, in a lot of cases, long before they are. If he can ensnare them while they're young, there's a good chance that he can have them for life.

The purpose of this book is to uncover and expose the snares of satan, making more and more believers aware of his strategies, schematic plots and twists so that they can see him coming and send him on his way. It says in Second Corinthians 2:11 (AMP), *"to keep Satan from taking advantage of us; for we are not ignorant of his schemes."* What good is having the victory in Christ and not knowing it? Or knowing it but being without the proper fortitude to wield it successfully? So you have victory...but if you can't access it, what good is it to you?

Most believers are familiar with Ephesians 6:12 (KJV), *"For we wrestle not against flesh and blood, but against principalities, against powers, against the rulers of darkness of this world, against spiritual wickedness in high places."* You, my fellow believer, are on the battleground; your life depends on your ability to remove the blindfolds and plainly see for yourself the forces at work against you. You are in a very real, intense invisible war for your soul. In this battle, you need to focus because it's either kill or be killed.

It's time for you to learn how to use your weapons so you can win every war. A fight is what Satan wants, and a fight is what he will get. No longer will we passively sit by and watch him run rampant throughout the pages of our lives. Why? Because we're being made aware of his tactics and are getting ourselves equipped to beat him at his own game. We are not fighting *for* the victory, Colossians 2:15 (NLT) teaches us: *"In this way, he disarmed the spiritual rulers and authorities.*

He shamed them publicly by his victory over them on the cross." When we learn this, we also understand that we are fighting *from* a place of victory.

Before we go any further, I want to lay out and make clear the intentions of Satan. He uses the same tactics in all areas— mind, flesh, and spirit—his tactics are the same, his approach and his techniques are what vary. He goes to great lengths to take us off course and use our hands to fulfill his missions. However, there is absolutely nothing he can do in the life of a Christian without God's permission; we learn this from the life of Job:

> *The Lord said to Satan, "Where have you come from?" Satan answered the Lord, "From roaming throughout the earth, going back and forth on it." Then the Lord said to Satan, "Have you considered by servant Job? There is no one on earth like him; he is blameless and upright, a man who fears God and shuns evil."*
>
> *"Does Job fear God for nothing?" Satan replied. "Have you not put a hedge around him and his household and everything he has? You have blessed the work of his hands, so that his flocks and herds are spread throughout the land. But now stretch out your hand and strike everything he has, and he will surely curse you to your face."*
>
> *The Lord said to Satan, "Very well, then, everything he has is in your power, but on the man himself do not lay a finger." Then Satan*

went out from the presence of the Lord (Job 1:7-12).

We see here that the enemy takes the time to survey the land searching for his next prey. And at times, God will cut his search short and give him exactly what it is he is looking for, but with clear-cut boundaries. It's safe to say that sometimes we are entered into battle, not because the enemy sought us out but because God volunteered us! Even still, with all of Satan's desires, strategies, intentions, and attempts, God remains the one in control; and as long as we belong to Him, the enemy of our souls will never have the last say. Let's explore six of his intentions and the Scriptures that fortify us against them.

1. SATAN DISTORTS YOUR VIEW OF GOD, THE FATHER

> *Then Jesus was led by the Spirit into the wilderness to be tempted by the devil. After fasting forty days and forty nights, he was hungry. The tempter came to him and said, "If you are the Son of God, tell these stones to become bread."*
>
> *Jesus answered, "It is written: 'Man shall not live on bread alone, but on every word that comes from the mouth of God.'"*
>
> *Then the devil took him to the holy city and had him stand on the highest point of the temple. "If you are the Son of God," he said, "throw yourself down. For it is written:*

'He will command his angels concerning you, and they will lift you up in their hands, so that you will not strike your foot against a stone.'"

Jesus answered him, "It is also written: 'Do not put the Lord your God to the test.'"

Again, the devil took him to a very high mountain and showed him all the kingdoms of the world and their splendor. "All this I will give you," he said, "if you will bow down and worship me."

Jesus said to him, "Away from me, Satan! For it is written: 'Worship the Lord your God, and serve him only.'"

Then the devil left him, and angels came and attended him (Matthew 4:1-11).

We know that the enemy's goal is to kill, steal, and destroy (John 10:10). What many of us do not know is that one of his main strategies for doing so is by causing us to think, perceive, and believe things about God that simply aren't true. As the father of lies, it's Satan's absolute pleasure to distort our view of God so that we can never fully know Him, embrace Him, or experience the depths of His love and plan for us. This is so important because once Satan is successful at distorting what we believe about God, he doesn't have to do much more to keep us separated from Him and the totality of the relationship He desires to have with us as His children. When we are unable to see Him as a loving, kind and generous Father, it makes it extremely difficult to receive His love, kindness, and generosity.

Neal T. Anderson, author of *Victory Over the Darkness* writes: "The major strategy of Satan is to distort the character of God and the truth of who we are. He can't change God and he can't do anything to change our identity and position in Christ. If, however, he can get us to believe a lie, we will live as though our identity in Christ isn't true."[1]

See, these misconceptions about God, birthed in us through various types of experiences, rob us of our ability to truly *"Love the Lord your God with all your heart and with all your soul and with all your strength and with all your mind"* (Luke 10:27). Although we know that God can never be totally understood by the human mind, the enemy's priority is to kill any part of us that would be willing to commit to a lifestyle of trying! John 8:44 tells us:

> *You belong to your father, the devil, and you want to carry out your father's desires. He was a murderer from the beginning, not holding to the truth, for there is no truth in him. When he lies, he speaks his native language, for he is a liar and the father of lies.*

This verse from God's Word, the Bible, puts everything into proper perspective, doesn't it? Because lying is his native language, you can expect that literally *everything* the devil says is untrue! The only truth he can speak is the Word of God; however, when he quotes the Word of God to you, you can expect that his motive is to get you to completely misinterpret or misunderstand its meaning. Once that happens, it's so easy for you to miss what God is saying and never receive the promises of the Scriptures.

As believers, it's so important that Satan does not know the Word of God better than we do, and even more important that we can discern his voice from our own and from the voice of our Father. If Jesus would have listened to Satan while in the wilderness, what would have been the outcome? See, his ability to steal, kill, and destroy becomes so much easier when what we believe about God is the opposite of who He is. Our distorted view has the power to keep us from accessing and tapping into the reservoir of heaven's pleasures and promises for us.

If you believe that you have a distorted view of God, I want to encourage you to surrender and submit those ideas and beliefs to the Father in prayer. One of the ways you can pinpoint whether or not your view of God has been tampered with and contaminated is your inability to receive Him as Father and expect Him to be just that. If this is you, allow the Holy Spirit to walk you through the truth of the Scriptures and to correct every wrong idea, thought, or belief concerning the Father.

John 8:32 says, *"Then you will know the truth, and the truth will set you free."* The only way to be made free is to *know* the truth. If you want to know the truth, you must allow the Holy Spirit to guide you. John 16:13 tells us, *"But when he, the Spirit of truth, comes, he will guide you into all the truth...."* Yield yourself, your mind, and your spirit to the Holy Spirit and be led into the truth.

The truth is, you are a child of God, not a slave. As His child, God wants the best for you; and when you truly understand this, it's only a matter of time before you will see, know it, and believe it.

*I will not leave you as orphans; I will come to
you* (John 14:18).

*The Spirit you received does not make you
slaves, so that you live in fear again; rather,
the Spirit you received brought about
your adoption to sonship. And by him we
cry, "Abba, Father." The Spirit himself testiѕ
fies with our spirit that we are God's children. Now if we are children, then we are
heirs—heirs of God and co-heirs with Christ,
if indeed we share in his sufferings in order
that we may also share in his glory* (Romans
8:15-17).

2. SATAN BREAKS YOUR WILL TO FIGHT SO HE CAN TAKE POSSESSION

*Finally, be strong in the Lord and in his mighty
power. Put on the full armor of God, so that
you can take your stand against the devil's
schemes. For our struggle is not against flesh
and blood, but against the rulers, against the
authorities, against the powers of this dark
world and against the spiritual forces of evil
in the heavenly realms. Therefore put on the
full armor of God, so that when the day of
evil comes, you may be able to stand your
ground, and after you have done everything,
to stand. Stand firm then, with the belt of
truth buckled around your waist, with the*

breastplate of righteousness in place, and with your feet fitted with the readiness that comes from the gospel of peace. In addition to all this, take up the shield of faith, with which you can extinguish all the flaming arrows of the evil one. Take the helmet of salvation and the sword of the Spirit, which is the word of God. And pray in the Spirit on all occasions with all kinds of prayers and requests. With this in mind, be alert and always keep on praying for all the Lord's people (Ephesians 6:10-18).

Satan understands that our battle is in the spirit; and he knows that if he can keep us from approaching the fight in the spirit, then he can keep us from our victory. Because many of us have a great grasp of this concept, we're not necessarily hesitant to engage in spiritual warfare. We know what it means to come into battle fully suited and ready to war. However, many believers don't always anticipate the many strategic ways the enemy comes to battle looking to strip us.

One by one, he looks to remove our weapons of warfare. What I mean is this—you started out fully suited, but now you're beginning to notice that your armor, piece by piece, is no longer secured or in place. Whether it's your belt that's no longer fastened, or your helmet that's no longer sitting upright, whatever it is, it's now evident that the enemy has been taking steps to strip you of what protects you.

You started out with your feet fitted with readiness, but now your feet are no longer as prepared as they once were. This is how the enemy slowly chips away at our full armor, and before we know it we are unwilling to continue in battle because we feel that the victory is now unattainable.

There is a level of confidence that comes to war with us when we are fully covered in our spiritual armor; but when the enemy begins to strip away at that armor, we begin to feel vulnerable and more susceptible to attack. No one wants to continue fighting in that condition. This is how Satan leaves us discouraged, distracted by our discouragement, and defeated. For this reason, it is imperative that we heed the instructions given. We must pray in the spirit on *all* occasions or as often as we can, and always remain alert. This will help us to adjust and readjust our armor however and whenever necessary. Being prayerful and alert at all times keeps us from being completely stripped of our armor and unable to wage a good warfare.

3. SATAN WEARS YOU DOWN TO GAIN CONTROL

The concepts discussed in number two are applicable here as well. When we find ourselves underdressed on the battlefield, it's so much easier for the enemy to tire us out. When he takes shots at our armor, we become too weak to fight back and thus he now has control. It's important that we routinely assess and evaluate the condition of our armor so that we are not caught on the battleground without adequate protection and nothing to pull from in order to fight back.

If you feel as though you are being worn down, I encourage you to immerse yourself in the word of God and in prayer all the more. Double up your devotional time if you have to, do whatever it takes to tighten up your armor.

You will keep in perfect peace those whose minds are steadfast, because they trust in you (Isaiah 26:3).

Never be lacking in zeal, but keep spiritual fervor, serving the Lord (Romans 12:11).

Whatever you do, work at it with all your heart, as working for the Lord, not for human masters (Colossians 3:23).

4. Satan Divides and Conquers

Satan loves to keep us divided, in constant quarrels, and at odds with one another because he knows that when we work together, he has no shot at taking us down. Being on a battlefield with a team of people who cannot work together has proven to be detrimental to success time and time again. It's almost equivalent to being in a war all by yourself even though you are surrounded by people.

It's simple, when we are divided, our enemy has the upper hand. Disunity weakens us as an army, which is the main reason the enemy loves to stir up dissension and discord among us so that we are unable to unify ourselves and work together to tear down his agenda. When we truly grasp this concept, we develop a keen eye for his tactics and are able to disarm him before his technique is successful. One of us can put one thousand to flight, but two of us can put ten thousand to flight (Deuteronomy 32:30), imagine what we can accomplish when armies of us, too many to be numbered, work together in the battle against the kingdom of darkness!

Satan is afraid of us ever truly understanding the power that comes to us when we become a unified body. He knows that if he doesn't divide and conquer us first, together we will have the power to divide and conquer his kingdom. It's vitally important that we recognize that we are on a battlefield and it's never about us, it's always about the plans of God being birthed on earth. Let's work together so that we can be the most powerful forces against all of hell!

> *Jesus knew their thoughts and said to them, "Every kingdom divided against itself will be ruined, and every city or household divided against itself will not stand"* (Matthew 12:25).

> *Again, truly I tell you that if two of you on earth agree about anything they ask for, it will be done for them by my Father in heaven. For where two or three gather in my name, there am I with them* (Matthew 18:19-20).

> *Do we not all have one Father? Did not one God create us? Why do we profane the covenant of our ancestors by being unfaithful to one another?* (Malachi 2:10)

> *How good and pleasant it is when God's people live together in unity!* (Psalm 133:1)

> *For just as each of us has one body with many members, and these members do not all have the same function, so in Christ we, though*

many, form one body, and each member belongs to all the others (Romans 12:4-5).

5. SATAN LOOKS FOR WINDOWS OF OPPORTUNITY

The enemy is *always* looking for a point of access into our hearts, our minds, and our spirits. It's not until he finds a way in that he can use us to fulfill his plans. It's our responsibility to do everything in our power to make sure he doesn't find those points of access by remaining fully submitted to God and committed to prayer. When we do these things, we are careful to never entertain His presence, and our spiritual senses will always alert us when the devil is lurking, looking for his next opportunity to advance.

> *And do not give the devil a foothold* (Ephesians 4:27).

> *Then it says, "I will return to the house I left." When it arrives, it finds the house unoccupied, swept clean and put in order* (Matthew 12:44).

6. SATAN FINDS YOUR WEAKNESSES AND EXPLOITS THEM

God was very purposeful and strategic when He created humans with weaknesses. Our weaknesses are what create in us a sobering and undying awareness of our ever-increasing need for Him. Scripture tells us there is absolutely nothing we can do without Him (John 15:5), but because we are not always quick to believe this, God left each of us with just enough human inabilities to keep us running to Him.

To exploit means to make full use of. God's plans for our weaknesses are the complete opposite of what Satan has planned for them. God loves to see His strength perfected in our weakness, whereas Satan loves to use our weaknesses to help defeat and destroy us. The enemy introduces to us feelings and thoughts of hopelessness with every one of our weaknesses in an effort to keep us from being able or willing to strengthen ourselves in that area. If he can convince us that our weakness is permanent, well, what sense is there in continuing to fight? He attempts to use one area of weakness to create others, and in doing so it's only a matter of time before he wins and we are defeated. Find your strength in the Word of God—and in those weak moments, remind yourself of what God said.

Finally, be strong in the Lord and in his mighty power. Put on the full armor of God, so that you can take your stand against the devil's schemes. For our struggle is not against flesh and blood, but against the rulers, against the authorities, against the powers of this dark world and against the spiritual forces of evil in the heavenly realms (Ephesians 6:10-12).

Beat your plowshares into swords and your pruning hooks into spears. Let the weakling say, "I am strong!" (Joel 3:10)

ENDNOTE

1. Neal T. Anderson, *Victory Over the Darkness* (Ventura, CA: Regal Books, 2013).

CHAPTER 2

![decorative bar]

TYPES OF BATTLEGROUNDS

I N THE UNITED STATES, THERE ARE SEVERAL BRANCHES of military:

- U.S. Army

- U.S. Marine Corps

- U.S. Navy

- U.S. Air Force

- U.S. Coast Guard

Though each are unique in their functions and over-all specialties, they all serve the same purpose—to protect and secure our country, and to some degree, they all must work together in order to be successful at doing so. We're not going to go into each of the different branches and their purposes, but what I want to point out here is that there is a ranking order for these systems, and they are each prepared and equipped for different types of battles on different battlegrounds.

Each branch requires different trainings and a different set of tools in order to effectively engage in the battle for their particular grounds. You can imagine that the Air Force is prepared to maintain security for our country above us while the Navy is prepared to secure our safety from beneath us. When an enemy seeks to take a stab at us from any direction, there's a system of security set in place that isn't easily breached and is purposely designed to keep that enemy from being able to enter. Although there have been times when the enemy has been able to breach those systems and gain access, it's rare, and each system is continuously striving to become stronger and more fortified day by day. Again, as it is in the natural, so it is in the spirit.

The following are the types of battlegrounds we will discuss:

- The Personal Battleground

- The Familial Battleground

For each, I will give a personal testimony of some things that I have walked through to give you a clear understanding of each scenario. For every type of battleground, a different set of skills and level of authority is necessary. Just like the Coast Guard is not purposely skilled or prepared to battle on land, we must create separate walls of defense in our prayer lives to ward off the enemy who wants to come at us from every angle. It's important to realize that while we are focused in one particular area, another is left unattended or wide open. The only way to do this is to pray without ceasing, constantly covering every area under the blood of Jesus. When we fail to remain prayerful, well, we are left unguarded and vulnerable to the attacks of Satan and his army.

THE PERSONAL BATTLEGROUND

I remember when I thought I was going to lose my mind for the third time. The enemy was constantly bullying me and tormenting me with negative thoughts concerning ministry. He told me over and over again that if I was to ever go forth in ministry, he'd attack different areas of my life such as my children, and that I'd never be able to go forth in the right state of mind. These suggestions were sent to instill fear in me; and although I knew these thoughts were the influence of demonic spirits, inwardly I began to entertain them. I began to consider the idea that quitting the ministry, walking away from deliverance, or no longer teaching or talking about spiritual warfare, that somehow this attack and assignment from hell on my life would end.

I started making internal resignations. These were things I never verbally expressed at the time; however, my actions began to reflect my inward truth—that I had quit. Internally, I found myself retreating and pulling back from doing certain things because I felt as though my doing so would make things easier for me. These internal resignations were a direct conflict for the will of God for my life.

One day, I specifically remember asking God, "Why won't this attack lift?" He said to me, "You've made internal resignations," and He began to bring to the surface those thoughts and the accompanying behaviors and actions that highlighted the ways in which I was slowly pulling back and resigning from the things that I was set on the earth to do. I sat on the sofa that day, and I can't remember whether or not I started to weep outwardly or inwardly, but I heard God ask me, "If you are not going to do what you were born to do, then why do you need to live?"

It was one of the most sobering questions He'd ever asked me. It was at that moment I realized that my purpose was much stronger than any attack of the enemy against me and I immediately began to break those internal resignations and come out of agreement with them. What I discovered was that these resignations were actual contracts, binding agreements that I made with Satan without even knowing it. I never said I would serve him or anything of that nature, but somehow I began to feel that if I agreed to the terms he was setting, he would stop pursuing me or fighting me so aggressively.

God reminded me in the middle of a powerful worship encounter that all of my fears, all of my doubts and concerns were irrelevant because He was the keeper of my soul, and if I could just learn again to trust Him, if I could learn again to see and believe Him to be the living God, the Savior, Jehovah Gibbor, the one who fights for me, then I would become victorious. This was probably one of the most intense battles I'd ever fought, but that moment made me feel like it was easy again. I began to trust God all over again as my Savior, my Redeemer, my Rescuer, my Mind Regulator. And all of a sudden, my fears and worries began to settle and I had the faith to live again.

Not soon after that attack, I crossed over the threshold and saw that I was closer to my destiny than I'd ever been, and I understood what the fight was all about. I remember ministering, while silently crossing this threshold. There was a power released that I never thought possible when Jesus Himself—the Deliverer—stepped into the room while I was preaching and many people began to give their lives to Christ, not because of me, but because of the revelation that I had grasped from the warfare that I'd just come out of victoriously.

As you can see, the personal battleground has everything to with our lives and those places where the enemy tries his hand at getting us to believe his lies and to no longer pursue the things God put in us. For many believers, these attacks are initiated in our childhood and consistently launched at us until we become aware of Satan's schemes and tactics. When you see yourself no longer desiring to actively engage with the will and purpose of God for your life—things you were once committed to and found enjoyment in—out of fear that the enemy is going to further attack you, your family, finances, or any other area of your life, that's when you know you're standing on a personal battleground. It's important you war in the spirit against this enemy by declaring the Word of God concerning you and refusing to pull back.

THE FAMILIAL BATTLEGROUND

On the familiar battleground is where we, as believers, have to exercise our authority and fight for our children, our spouses, and our families as a whole. Here, I want to emphasize the importance of fighting for your children. Parental authority is greater than any other authority in the earth as it relates to our kids. There have been many situations where I've personally had to war on behalf of my own.

One occurrence in particular was with my son who played sports. He had a dream of attending a university to play professional ball; however, because he did not focus enough on his academics, he was forced to settle for a junior college. At this time, there was a particular college that was accepting young men and when they accepted my son, I didn't have any peace about it and I didn't understand why. There was something the Holy Spirit was trying to warn me about, but I didn't yet have the details. One day, I went to sleep and I had a dream.

Although I am a dreamer and accustomed to dreaming, this particular time I went into part of the dream realm that was unfamiliar to me, a place I've not been before. I initially thought this dream was a side effect of a medication I was taking at the time, but I would soon understand that it wasn't related to that at all and that God was indeed trying to show me something.

So, in this dream, I saw from beginning to end through prophetic symbolism, a situation that would soon occur in real life. The Holy Spirit walked me through the college campus and allowed me to plainly see everything that was happening there, from the different types of perversion to the idol worship and all things in between. At the very end of this dream, a cell phone appeared in my hand. My son was calling and when I answered, I immediately asked him if he was okay, his response was "No."

I woke up from the dream and I just couldn't shake it. I was deeply troubled and I just knew that if my son were to attend this school there would be a situation that would bring him to the point of rage and it would be extremely difficult to get him out of it. When I woke up, I didn't need paper or pen. I can, even still, recite the entire dream, detail by detail.

During my travels one weekend, my husband took our son to tour the campus. I was disturbed, uneasy, and overwhelmingly anxious because I vividly saw in the spirit the details and could readily anticipate what was getting ready to happen. My husband tried to assure me that nothing was wrong and that it was a nice campus; and despite my anxiety, I asked them to call me when they arrived. When he called, I begin to describe the front of the building to him just as I saw it in my dream. I asked him if my description was accurate and he told me yes. At this point, I was certain that God was showing me something; I tried to convince my son not to go, but he was already so fixated on going away for college and being able to play football that he did not listen. Because his father is not necessarily a dreamer as I am, he didn't understand the total weight that I was carrying as it related to this dream and this school.

Note: The following may be uncomfortable for you to read as it contains very sensitive information regarding racism and unjust circumstances.

Before my son was scheduled to leave for school, I had another dream that showed me three men. In this dream, there was one detective, one police officer, and one other man who was good with computers. I was sitting in a room where these men were interrogating me about my son. At the end, the same cell phone that appeared in my first dream appeared, and I called my husband to tell him that our son was in trouble. When I woke up, I knew that I had to pray specifically concerning these three men.

Now it's moving day. We get to this campus and as I looked around, a lot of what I saw in the spirit could not be confirmed naturally. The people were nice, his roommates seemed nice, but what I did notice was a stillness—almost as if the presence of God wasn't there. There was no confirmation from the Holy Spirit that he should be there.

Six weeks into the semester, my son is doing well and maintaining As when a young lady invites him to a party. We had rules that he wouldn't attend any parties without us meeting parents and things of that nature, but this young lady invites him to a party and he feels good about it and he decides to attend. Once he arrives, he notices that he is the only African American in attendance and soon finds himself surrounded by a bunch of racist teenage boys.

He, along with a friend who accompanied him, tried to stand his ground and explain that he was invited by a young lady to this party. These young men insisted that they leave because there were "no niggers allowed" and began to taunt them with other names. Eventually things got out of control, loud, and rowdy and the police were called to break up the party. My son and his friend walked in one direction and the boys went another.

Before long, the young men, about ten of them, decided to turn back and follow my son and his friend until they circled them. My son's first instinct was to do something to get away from these boys, so he hit one and ran, with his friend running behind him. He didn't know that the young man was intoxicated and that once he hit him, he'd fall and hit his face.

This young man's father was part of the Masons who ruled the town, and as a result of this incident, there would be an extensive, uphill battle he'd now have to face. The young man's father, without any investigation, made one phone call and my son was arrested and charged with first-degree assault, thrown out of school, and all of his scholarships, grants, and aid were revoked. His dream went down the drain. Before long, the local newspapers had his full name and face in print, painting him to be a criminal.

Now it was time for me to go to war. Although I had been praying intensely since having those two dreams, at this point, I understood I needed to go to war to fight for my son or this enemy would gain the victory over him, leaving his faith and future shattered. When I started praying, it was as if God had etched the details of those dreams in my mind in such a way that I would be constantly reminded and unwilling to relent or pull back from prayer.

A few days following his expulsion and his criminal charges, he had to go back to the school. I drove him there, and when we arrived, there were three men who got out of a car beside the building, and I immediately recognized these men from my second dream. As we're pulling around to the back of the building, I began to explain to my son who these men are, what their roles would be going forward, and which one would be trying to pin the charges on him, before he formally met them.

Long story short, when we were inside, before the men could introduce themselves to me, I was able to tell them who they were one by one according to what God revealed to me in my dream. They then took my son into a room where they proceeded to aggressively interrogate him, literally trying to force him to admit to a crime he didn't commit. I went into the room with my husband on speaker phone, and it was quite evident to me that they didn't like that I had my husband present with me on the phone. I believe this is what settled them all the way down, as they were sobered by the reality that there was a man in our lives—that my son's father was an active parent. I told them that their interrogation was now to end until my son was given adequate legal representation as he was entitled.

Although in that moment I was speaking concerning the natural, I knew that I was also referring to his representation in the spirit. I was aware that this battle was both happening in the natural and in the spirit realm over my son's destiny; and because I was his mother, it was up to me to use my parental authority to begin to dismantle and overturn these spiritual barricades that were set against my son by hell.

Finally, my son was formally charged with first-degree assault while the other young men who were involved weren't charged with anything at all as we were told that their actions and their threats had no bearings on the case. We then cleared out his dorm room and went home where I began to aggressively seek the proper legal representation to assist us with the upcoming hearings.

We found a lawyer who agreed to take the case and my husband became the primary contact for him. The attorney interviewed my son and felt strongly that he could win the case. Between him leaving the school and his court hearing, I spent a great amount of time in prayer interceding for him and asking God to intervene. It was clear to me that we were dealing with high-ranking demonic spirits and that we needed to take this matter into the courts of heaven and stand before the righteous Judge who would judge these matters justly. We needed God to work on our behalf. There are some cases that can only be won by God Himself.

Two days before the hearing, I was anxiously praying for God to give us justice and telling Him what we needed as if He didn't already know. I remember asking God if this wasn't going to work in our favor, to please give us a miracle. The day before the scheduled hearing, we were told that it was postponed. Initially, I was so upset about this until the Holy Spirit settled me and told me that He was working through this and on our behalf. The matter was postponed for six weeks later and my husband accompanied our son to court.

When they stepped into the courtroom, the defendant and his father were completely flabbergasted and whispering among one another, "That's his father!" as if they were astonished and in disbelief that his father was actually present. Finally, the attorney greeted them and introduced them to the judge and proceeded to have a discussion with the opposing counsel.

When he returned to my husband and son, he informed them that there had been a change of heart of the defendant's father and that he no longer wanted to press charges. Instead, he petitioned the courts to issue my son a fine for $500 and to simply take time to consider what he had done; all of the other charges were dropped.

When both attorneys submitted these updates to the judge, let's just say he was bewildered and confused. The judge couldn't wrap his mind around what had just taken place, but we understood completely. We knew that the righteous Judge stepped in on our behalf and changed the heart of that father. We understood that during those six weeks, God was working on this man's heart. Scripture tells us that the heart of the king is in the hand of the Lord, and He turns it however He wants.

Familial battlegrounds are all too familiar and common for believers. When Satan can't get hold of us because of our commitment to remain faithful and consistent in prayer, he will always attack the closest thing to us. Just as we discussed concerning the personal battlegrounds, do not allow the enemy to cause you to cease fire and retreat out of fear of what his next move is. With the Word of God, we have been well-equipped for any and every type of dagger the devil can launch. Don't be afraid; stand your ground! Go to war for your children! War for your spouse! War for your family! *War!* Their destiny may be at stake and *you* have the power to bruise Satan's head and cause him to lay down his weapons.

PRAYER AND CONFESSION

Father, in the name of Jesus,
I decree and declare that I walk in strong discern-
ment and I have 20/20 vision in the spirit. I am
focused and I am obtaining insight concerning

my destiny daily. I decree and declare that I am never caught off guard; You are downloading battle strategies into me ahead of time, in Jesus' name. I am always one step ahead of the enemy and I have full strength for every battle. I bind battle fatigue and release a fresh wind anointing, in Jesus' name.

God, help me to fight battles in season. Help me to always discern time wasters and useless battles that come to cause premature exhaustion. God, You are the leader of every fight, You go before me and will ensure that I win, every time! Thank You for never bringing me to a battle that You intend for me to lose. I believe that I am always guaranteed the victory as long as You are with me.

Jehovah Gibbor, You are the God of war. I carry your DNA, and I decree and declare that the warrior within is rising, and I am determined to win. I make full use of my weapons; I am dressed for battle and have all that I need. I decree and declare that this battleground is not bigger than me because it is God who fights for me! The devil is defeated because Jesus has already given us the victory through the work of the cross—and because of this, I always win!

BATTLEGROUND NUMBER ONE

WINNING THE WAR
IN THE MIND

CHAPTER 3

STRONGHOLDS IN THE MIND

IT'S NO SECRET—SATAN ALWAYS TARGETS THE MINDS OF believers. It is now and has always been his primary point of attack. I'm sure many are familiar with the term "the battlefield of the mind," right? We've heard it here and there constantly over the past two decades especially. The reason it hasn't faded with time is because people, both believers and non-believers alike, are becoming increasingly aware of the struggle 100 percent of the population has in their psyche.

There's no getting around it! We are constantly bombarded with thoughts and images of every kind that are released through the world system, which is controlled by the devil. He is sometimes more aware than we are that if he has control of our minds, then of course, he can have control of our bodies. If he can control our thinking, he can control our decisions; with that, his agenda is being fulfilled throughout the earth—through *us!*

Think about it. When your mind is taken captive and controlled by Satan, how can you fulfill the plans and purposes of God for your life? God has plans for you and so does the enemy; who you yield your mind and all of your faculties to will determine whose plans unfold in your life.

Dismantling Mental Torment

Throughout Scripture we have examples of the targeted mind games and tricks of the enemy that have us up and down in our beliefs, our perceptions, our perspectives, and our overall sense of well-being. We must start here because if we don't find stability in our minds, there's no possible way we will be able to get our flesh and our spirits under control. This evil spirit comes to exhaust us mentally and impair us physically, ultimately keeping us from fulfilling our assigned purpose for being here.

Mental torment is one of the biggest, if not, *thee* biggest, most powerful weapon hell routinely launches against the body of believers. Torment is defined as severe mental suffering, agony, distress, or *torture.* It is designed to leave us emotionally unstable, incapable of making right decisions, fearful, anxious, and spiritually paralyzed. There are countless men and woman of God bound by this spirit and don't even know it!

I know firsthand because I can remember a time in my own journey when this dastardly spirit gained undeniable access to my mind and I couldn't figure out how to break free. During that time, what I discovered is that this spirit is highly oppressive and distinguishably overwhelming; it appears to have only one job—to harass you and bring you to a place where peace is unable to penetrate and inhabit. Simply put: where there is mental torment, there is the absence of peace, and where there is the absence of peace, there is the absence of the presence of God!

I'm not speaking of the omnipresent existence of God here. I don't want to confuse you. What I am specifically referring to is the feeling and sensing of His presence, the presence that affirms and assures us that He is with us. This is the presence that doesn't require faith. See, where there is no peace, it is almost impossible to muster up the faith to continue on your journey toward victory.

Peace is a promise. It is a gift from God to the believers whose trust is in Him and whose minds are stayed on Him (Isaiah 26:3). The only way for us to gain access to and maintain the peace God promises to us, our minds must be submitted to Him at all times. Once our minds are submitted to and stayed on Him, we are able to rest safe and secure in the promise of Romans 16:20, "*The God of peace will soon crush Satan under your feet. The grace of our Lord Jesus be with you.*" This helps us to consistently pursue His presence totally convinced that He has us on His mind and that everything that concerns us concerns Him.

The Bible states, "'*There is no peace,*' says the Lord, '*for the wicked*'" (Isaiah 48:22; 57:21). As a believer, that does not include you! Therefore, peace is your portion and all it requires is that you decide, choose that it is indeed something you want and God will not withhold it from you (Psalm 84:11). However, you have to be willing to apply the Scriptures—in whole, not in part—to your mind.

James 4:7 tells us to *"Submit yourselves, then, to God. Resist the devil, and he will flee from you."* To submit means to yield or surrender to the power, will and/or authority of another. Some expositors even go as far as to define it as a personal resignation, which signifies individuals' willingness to remove themselves from any prior position of control or power as they employ and literally *give themselves over* to someone higher than them. I find that to be extremely powerful!

This Scripture verse in James 4 is purely conditional; and as such, it is extremely important for us as sons and daughters of God to not just understand, but to fully embrace just how powerful submission to God truly is and how impossible it is for us to win any war without it. Submission is a prerequisite for winning any victory as it is the very thing that gives us the power to resist the devil, causing him to flee.

When we fail to submit ourselves to God, the enemy is able to overpower us and take advantage of us. When we submit to God, we're actually stepping into the strength of God, we step into a total reliance upon God that gives us all of the power we need; then and only then does God become bigger than the enemy in our eyes. You see, he appears to be bigger than us only when we look at things from a natural perspective, because in the natural we have limited resources and limited access to the supernatural.

A great many believers have not yet tapped into one of our most powerful resources, that is the massive army God has assigned to us to protect us. I want to encourage you— *you have help!* Let's look at the life of Daniel for a moment:

> *Just then a hand touched me and lifted me, still trembling, to my hands and knees. And the man said to me, "Daniel, you are very precious to God, so listen carefully to what I have to say to you. Stand up, for I have been sent to you." When he said this to me, I stood up, still trembling.*
>
> *Then he said, "Don't be afraid, Daniel. Since the first day you began to pray for understanding and to humble yourself before your God, your request has been heard in heaven. I have come in answer to your prayer. But for twenty-one days the spirit prince of the kingdom of Persia blocked my way. Then Michael, one of the archangels, came to help me, and I left him there with the spirit prince of the kingdom of Persia. Now I am here to explain what will happen to your people in the future, for this vision concerns a time yet to come."*
>
> *While he was speaking to me, I looked down at the ground, unable to say a word. Then the one who looked like a man touched my lips, and I opened my mouth and began to speak. I said to the one standing in front of me, "I am filled with anguish because of the vision I have seen, my lord, and I am very weak. How can*

someone like me, your servant, talk to you, my lord? My strength is gone, and I can hardly breathe."

Then the one who looked like a man touched me again, and I felt my strength returning. "Don't be afraid," he said, "for you are very precious to God. Peace! Be encouraged! Be strong!"

As he spoke these words to me, I suddenly felt stronger and said to him, "Please speak to me, my lord, for you have strengthened me."

He replied, "Do you know why I have come? Soon I must return to fight against the spirit prince of the kingdom of Persia, and after that the spirit prince of the kingdom of Greece will come. Meanwhile, I will tell you what is written in the Book of Truth. (No one helps me against these spirit princes except Michael, your spirit prince)" (Daniel 10:10-21 NLT).

This is a powerful example of what it means to pray and not see your answer right away. Daniel had to wait twenty-one days, which to many of us these days is an excessive amount of time! It's important that we understand this. Daniel's prayers were heard, but his answer was being blocked. Many of us pray for the same things again and again, worrying that God hasn't heard us when there are times when what we've asked for is on its way, we just have to employ our angels to go to war on our behalf and get them to us.

Daniel's answer was being blocked by the Prince of Persia, that's no small plight! But just like the angel said to Daniel,

"Do not be afraid," we need not worry! God has given His angels a job and that is to assist His sons and daughters in battle. Hebrews 1:14 (AMP) makes it clear for us what their role is in our lives, *"Are not all the angels ministering spirits sent out [by God] to serve (accompany, protect) those who will inherit salvation? [Of course they are!]."*

Angels are employed by God and sent out to serve us. When we don't know this, the enemy has the power to intimidate us and scare us out of receiving our inheritance. Satan is a bully. His demonic spirits are bullies and they do have some level of power; however, they are not now, nor will they ever be, more powerful than the children of God. We have the Holy Spirit living inside us that gives us power over the enemy—all we need to do is access and exercise the authority given to us as the sons and daughters of God.

Psalm 103:20-21 (NLT) says, *"Praise the Lord, you angels, you mighty ones who carry out his plans, listening for each of his commands. Yes, praise the Lord, you armies of angels who serve him and do his will!"* Again, I want to encourage you— you have help. God was mindful of you when He created these angelic armies that are able to aide us in war and protect us from the attempts of the enemy to destroy us.

I'd like to end this chapter with this thought. Whenever you are in a mental battle, there is a cause—and it is important that you take the time to discover what it is. In most cases, wherever you find torment, you will find the spirit of fear. These spirits actually coexist. When you think about it, fear is the absence of peace. It is uncertainty, doubt, the lack of trust and utter confusion.

The enemy does not have a right to torment us unless we give it to him. Once we become aware of this, we can take back our power and the enemy has to release his hold, our freedom leaves him with no other choice. As sons and daughters of God, it is only when we are liberated from this bullying spirit of torture that our peace literally torments hell and shreds its agenda—not only for our lives, but also for the lives assigned to us. If you ever want to torture the enemy of your soul, *find the peace of God and walk in it!* All of the tools and strategies needed in order for you to do so are provided and thoroughly laid out for you throughout the next few chapters.

CHAPTER 4

RETRAINING YOUR
THOUGHTS

D R. CAROLINE LEAF, IN HER BOOK *THINK, LEARN, SUCceed,* says the following: "It has been collectively demonstrated that just about every aspect of our thinking, learning, and intelligence—our brainpower—can be improved by intense, targeted, deliberate mind training. In short, hard work and deep thinking are essential to success in life."[1] If we'd take the time to make intentional investments into our "power center," we can drastically improve all other parts of our lives.

The truth is, your thoughts are what create and determine your reality. In other words, I can look at the condition your life is in and develop a pretty good sense of what you have been thinking and meditating on, that's how powerful our minds are! You have the power to create your future by taking control of your thoughts today. You are probably familiar with the Scripture that says, *"For as he thinks in his heart, so is he"* (Proverbs 23:7 NKJV). For this reason, it's so important that we make every effort to transform, improve, and strengthen our minds and hearts so we can prepare ourselves for the futures God designed for us before we were even born. Our thoughts can lead us into His promises or away from them.

You can think yourself into weakness or you can think yourself into strength, it's up to you which way you choose to go. Our thoughts, whether healthy or unhealthy, are our responsibility. Let's examine three ways, or strategies, we can use to retrain our minds to think the way God would have us think.

1. STUDY THE SCRIPTURES

If you get an arsenal of weapons in your hand and you do nothing with them, how do they benefit you? What fruit will that bear? Not using your weapons leaves you defenseless, powerless, and ultimately, defeated. I've counseled many people under different types of attacks in their lives and one of the first questions I always lead with is, *"What has God said?"* or *"Are you reading God's Word?"* I have personally been shifted by the power of the *written* word, the power of the *spoken* word, and the power of the *prophetic* word many, many times. I ask individuals whether or not they have been listening for God's word for them—as it has the power to retrain us. It has the power to debunk every lie that the enemy speaks to us.

I remember times when I couldn't find the strength within me to pick up my physical Bible.

During those times, the Holy Spirit would instruct me to listen to the teachings of certain Bible teachers. These teachings would sustain me, temporarily, through seasons of war and those moments when I found it difficult to indulge in the Word of God for myself. Romans 10:17 encourages us: *"Consequently, faith comes from hearing the message, and the message is heard through the word about Christ."*

When I took the time to listen to the spoken or preached word of God, it was only a matter of time before I felt my faith being restored, my inner strength increase, and my appetite for the word of God being stirred once again. I want to be clear—by no means is this an excuse for anyone to purposely or perpetually replace their personal study of the Bible with listening to the spoken word. However, it is a viable tool that can be utilized when hell's assignment against you has you in a weakened state. The amount of time you remain in this weakened condition is totally up to you.

The Word of God is *"...quick, and powerful, and sharper than any twoedged sword, piercing even to the dividing asunder of soul and spirit, and of the joints and marrow, and is a **discerner of the thoughts** and intents of the heart"* (Hebrews 4:12 KJV). And Romans 1:16 (KJV) says, *"For I am not ashamed of **the gospel of Christ**: for it is the **power of God** unto salvation to every one that believeth; to the Jew first, and also to the Greek."* What this means to me is that God's Word not only ushers people into receiving Christ, but it also has the power to sustain them until the completed work of salvation is fully manifested in their lives.

Jesus makes it vividly clear to us when He says in Matthew 4:4: *"It is written: 'Man shall not live on bread alone, but on every word that comes from the mouth of God.'"* If we want to live, *truly* live, we cannot do so without the Word of God. This verse does not do away with our very natural need for food; however, it makes plain our need for this other, vitally important source that we cannot go too long without—again, that is if we want to truly live. Being malnourished in the natural has the potential to kill us, but being malnourished in the spirit? We are slowly dying. Let me explain.

Having an appetite for the Word of God and digesting it daily is what fortifies us and gives us the wherewithal to stand amid attacks and not lose our footing. Too many believers make it a priority to fulfill their natural cravings and fail to create, maintain, or satisfy spiritual cravings, which is the only way to stand against the woes of the devil. Let's look a little deeper.

Cravings do not just appear out of nowhere. They are created in us, and by us. What many people do not know is that our cravings can be both selective and nonselective. They are natural responses to our bodies from the parts of our brain that house and store our memories and pleasure sensors. A selective craving is only created once people have *tasted* a thing and *enjoyed* it. Their brains will automatically store that memory and stir up strong, unrelenting desires within them for that very thing from time to time. Of course, this can be both for good things and the not-so-good things, you know, those guilty pleasures!

On the other hand, nonselective cravings are caused by our deficiencies. They can be considered what I like to call an inner alarm system, where our bodies scream at us—literally through our cravings—when we are lacking certain needed and very necessary nutrients, even if it is just water at times. In many cases, we are completely unaware that our bodies are lacking until our cravings kick in to let us know.

These nonselective cravings stir up such strong hunger pangs within us, for example, until we are willing to eat *anything* for a bit of relief. The only way to get rid of a craving is to satisfy it. What this means is that these types of cravings do not require anything specific, but it will send you on a warpath, consuming everything in sight until your body is no long deficient in whatever nutrient you were lacking. Can you see where I'm going with this? As it is in the natural, so it is in the spirit!

As you can probably imagine, we definitely want to increase those selective cravings and decrease the nonselective ones when it comes to our spiritual lives. Those selective cravings are based on an appetite filled with the Word of God and actually finding pleasure in it. When we get to the point where we actually enjoy reading the Scriptures and we are no longer doing so out of responsibility, we'll find ourselves craving more and more of it until our spirit simply cannot get by without it. Again, this can only occur once we have already tasted and found enjoyment and pleasure in the Word of God.

Dealing with the nonselective cravings, it is so important that we develop such an appetite for the Word of God so that our spirit is not found lacking vital nutrients too often.

We don't want to get rid of our inner alarm system, but what we need to do is reduce the number of times it is forced to sound off. In this instance, our cravings are synonymous with our convictions. These convictions tap us on the shoulder every now and again to alert us that our spirits haven't been adequately fed, and as a result, are now deficient of the necessities needed to continue.

I told you that when these nonselective cravings kick in, people are willing to consume anything to relieve themselves from the constant nagging of those ravenous cravings. This is extremely dangerous! Those being led by these cravings will find themselves at a table set by the enemy, consuming his deceitful crumbs one by one. Because nothing he can offer them has any substance or nutritional value, those deficiencies are not being dealt with, which causes the cravings to continue and keeping them in a perpetual cycle where they return to his table again and again to temporarily calm their cravings.

But, there's a simple fix for both: to increase your selective cravings, you need more and more of the Word of God! And to decrease the nonselective cravings, you need more and more of the Word of God! Matthew 5:6 says, *"Blessed are those who hunger and thirst for righteousness, for they will be filled."* This verse is a binding agreement, an absolute guarantee to us from God. When we develop an appetite for the things of God, He promises that we will be filled.

Part of the reason so many believers do not reap the benefits and rewards of this powerful tool is simply because they choose to live *defensively* as opposed to *offensively*. What this means is that many wait until they are in the middle of an intense mind battle before they start consuming the Scriptures and fighting back—instead of preparing for the battle proactively, while they're in a strong headspace. Preparing ahead of time fortifies us, giving us ample grounds to gird ourselves for what we *know* is forthcoming.

See, what we know is that the enemy is going to try us over and over again until we surrender these earthly bodies. What we also know is that in Christ we have victory. In those between times, those times of war, however, we sometimes need to be reminded. Here's a couple of thoughts: You will never see a soldier preparing for a battle on the battleground! You will never see a soldier dressing for the battle in front of his enemy! These steps are taken care of beforehand.

Most people get dressed in private, right? This is important because when it is time for war, we shouldn't be *getting* ready, we should *be* ready. Matthew 24:44 says, *"So you also must be ready, because the Son of Man will come at an hour when you do not expect him."* Just like we can expect Christ to return at any given moment, we can expect the enemy to show up looking for a fight at any given moment. As believers, the question is never "will" we fight, the question is always "when." The enemy will always roar like a lion seeking whomever he can devour—but when you're equipped with the Word of God as your most powerful resource, that toothless lion will never devour you! I encourage you, stay in God's Word and you will win every time!

2. VERBALLY DECLARE THE SCRIPTURES

The demonic realm gains its momentum and strategies for access to our lives and minds through the gateway of deceit.

One of the quickest and easiest entry points into our spirits is through our own mouths! Our words are either the key that locks the door behind our tormentor or opens the door giving him permission to enter. When we confess things that are contrary to the Word of God, the enemy grabs hold of those negative words and uses them against us as he knocks down our walls of defense and lodges himself and his beliefs within us. Isn't that crazy? He finds all of the strength he needs through our own confessions and then he uses them to separate us from the solid and sure foundation established for us in Christ. Let's break this down further.

> **A MIND THAT ISN'T FULL OF THE WORD OF GOD HAS ENTIRELY TOO MUCH ROOM FOR EVERYTHING CONTRARY.**

A mind that isn't full of the Word of God has entirely too much room for everything contrary. With your mind on all things outside of the Word of God, there's no doubt that your speech, your declarations, and your conversations will all reflect that. Why? Because that's what you've been meditating on and entertaining. Philippians 4:8 tells us:

> *Finally, brothers and sisters, whatever is true, whatever is noble, whatever is right, whatever is pure, whatever is lovely, whatever is admirable—if anything is excellent or praiseworthy, think about such things.*

I'm sure you are aware of how difficult it is for anyone to think one thing and say another, in doing so we find ourselves tripping over our words and having to repeat ourselves or stop altogether and try to voice our thoughts from the beginning, with clarity. Another example is in writing. Have you ever found yourself sitting down to write something and being interrupted by a conversation completely unrelated? What I am getting at is how difficult it is for us as a people to focus our minds on one thing while saying or doing something contrary or unrelated. It's almost impossible, and understandably so!

A mind filled with the Word of God will be accompanied by a mouth that constantly speaks the Word of God. Joshua 1:8 says:

> *Keep this Book of the Law **always** on your lips; meditate on it day and night, so that you may be careful to do everything written in it. Then you will be prosperous and successful.*

So even when your thoughts try to take you off course and into those places that weren't designed for you, we see here that speaking the Word of God out loud has the power to arrest those thoughts and steer them back into proper alignment, literally adjusting your mindset. Proverbs 18:20 tells us, *"From the fruit of their mouth a person's stomach is filled; with the harvest of their lips they are satisfied."* Doesn't this verse put things into perspective? Your mouth has the power to leave you full and satisfied—or empty and longing. And we've already talked about where being empty and longing can take us!

Furthermore, declaring the Scriptures out loud has the power to change any atmosphere! I don't care what is going on around you or within you, when you begin to decree the Word of God out of your mouth, you are literally taking captive any force in your surrounding space that opposes and hinders an atmosphere of freedom and the presence of God. John 1:1 says, *"In the beginning was the Word, and the Word was with God, and the Word was God."* This makes it so painstakingly clear to us that God and His Word are one and cannot be separated; so when you embrace His Word and allow it to come out of your mouth, what you are actually doing is releasing God into your atmosphere. Does that make sense? The same way we are able to usher the enemy into our space with our negative words, we can usher the presence of God into our space with His Word. With His Word comes His presence!

Fill your mind with the thoughts of God and your words will undoubtedly change, which will in turn, change your life! Yes, our mouths are that powerful. Practice this, His Word will not let you down.

3. RECORD AND REHEARSE PERSONAL PROPHETIC PROMISES

Let's jump right in here! First Timothy 1:18-19 in the King James Version of the Bible says:

> *This charge I commit unto thee, son Timothy,*
> *according to the prophecies which went before*
> *on thee, that though by them mightiest war*
> *a good warfare; holding faith, and a good*

conscience; which some having put away concerning faith have made shipwreck.

The New Living Translation of the Bible puts it like this:

Timothy, my son, here are my instructions for you, based on the prophetic words spoken about you earlier. May they help you fight well in the Lord's battles. Cling to your faith in Christ, and keep your conscience clear. For some people have deliberately violated their consciences; as a result, their faith has been shipwrecked.

WOW!

Prophetic words and promises are a life-giving tool that God gives us sometimes directly, and other times through His chosen and trusted vessels being led by the Holy Spirit. I have personally learned just how incredibly useful this can be in seasons of war. I can remember plenty of times when I would replay and listen to the prophetic words spoken over my life, which served as a powerful tool that diverted the very lies of the enemy and helped tremendously to retrain my thinking.

As life unfolds, it's so easy to forget what God has promised you, this is why having prophetic moments recorded and stored can save you in times of intense battle. When you remind yourself of the prophetic promises spoken to you by God, you are forced to consider what His thoughts are concerning you, your current condition, and your future conditions. It empowers you, undergirds you, and gives you a refreshed sense of self, which is essential when you are in battle.

I remember negative words that were spoken over me when I was a little girl, specifically an instance when my father told me that I'd never amount to anything when I refused to do something he asked of me because I didn't agree. Those words always seemed to resurface in pivotal moments—the times when I found myself thriving, in those times when my efforts were being met with success, or when I was striving and making significant advances. Those words spoken to me during my childhood would, without my permission, begin to replay in my mind.

The prophetic word of God has the power to uproot every word that Satan himself, the father of lies, has planted. The prophetic word in and of itself is a root planted within us that gives us a keen sense of insight and foreknowledge concerning our futures. One of Satan's strategies is to cause weeds to grow around the prophetic words planted in you so that he can suck them dry.

For me, the weeds were those negative words planted in my soul in my youth. Weeds, in the natural, are always at war with the thing intentionally planted as they compete for water, sunlight, and other nutrients needed for growth. Gardeners are quick to pluck them out because they grow so rapidly, leaving the actual plants stifled and unable to grow.

That's how it is spiritually, as well. If we allow one weed, just one, to grow without plucking it out, we can expect that in no time at all, we'll have an army full of weeds literally choking the life out of our prophetic promises until we are unable to recall them or rehearse them. The problem with this is that our expectations become dangerously impaired. How can we expect from God things we can't remember He promised us? This doesn't mean that these promises will never come to pass, but it does mean that they can be seriously delayed. The enemy has the ability to prolong our times of war because we lack the wherewithal to reroute his lies with the truth of God's promises to us.

Allow me to insert a quick sidebar here. There are times when we are in jeopardy of not seeing the fulfillment of the prophetic word over our lives because, like Moses, we fail to follow instructions. Numbers 20:6-12 (NLT) says:

> *Moses and Aaron turned away from the people and went to the entrance of the Tabernacle, where they fell face down on the ground. Then the glorious presence of the Lord appeared to them, and the Lord said to Moses, "You and Aaron must take the staff and assemble the entire community. As the people watch, speak to the rock over there, and it will pour out its water. You will provide enough water from the rock to satisfy the whole community and their livestock."*
>
> *So Moses did as he was told. He took the staff from the place where it was kept before the Lord. Then he and Aaron summoned the people to come and gather at the rock. "Listen, you rebels!" he shouted. "Must we bring you water from this rock?" Then Moses raised his hand and struck the rock twice with the staff,*

*and water gushed out. So the entire commu-
nity and their livestock drank their fill.*

*But the Lord said to Moses and Aaron,
"Because you did not trust me enough to
demonstrate my holiness to the people of
Israel, you will not lead them into the land I
am giving them!"*

Moses lost out on seeing the fulfillment of his prophetic
promise because he allowed his momentary frustration to
lead him into deliberate disobedience to the instructions
of God. Instead of speaking to the rock, he chose to strike
it. We all have moments like these; however, we are not
always aware of the consequences these moments can yield
and what they can cost us in totality. Moses had a temporary setback, I'm sure if he knew what it would cost him he
would've chosen differently. When God spoke to him, he
said, *"Because you didn't trust me enough...."* How many times
do we make hasty decisions against God's instructions out of
our lack of trust? Seeing the fulfillment of prophecy not only
requires us to make our constant decrees and declarations—
it also requires our obedience.

Your prophetic promises from God and those negative
words of the enemy will only be at war until you learn how
to rehearse one over the other. To rehearse your prophetic
promises is to make a conscious effort to recite or repeat
what God said as often as you need to in order to keep yourself reminded and in expectation of their fulfillment. Of
course Satan would rather us recite his lies over God's truths,
but the decision is ours on which one we will give the upper
hand to by our repeated declarations. Although my father

is forgiven now, those word curses still, at times, attempt to exercise authority over me. However, the power of the prophetic words and deliverance help nullify the power of the negative words so that they cannot and will not manifest.

Many of us have healthy roots planted by prophetic words and unhealthy roots planted by the enemy. The prophetic word, when released and then rehearsed, has the power to uproot those negative words and reverse them. For this reason, I record prophetic words. I also track them so that I can make note of when they come to pass and continue to war over the ones I am still waiting to see come to fruition. Because I believe the Source of each prophetic promise is the Holy Spirit, I am assured that if I pray and continue to war over those words through the power of decrees and declarations, I can watch in anticipation and expect to see them come to pass. This is called stewarding the prophetic word. Jeremiah 1:12 tells us, *"The Lord said to me, 'You have seen correctly, for I am watching to see that my word is fulfilled.'"* When God speaks a thing, it will surely come to pass!

I want to be clear, rehearsing our prophetic promises alone does not guarantee us the victory; however, it does highlight the devotion of God to assuring that His words will come to pass in our lives. This is why it is so essential that we partner with Him in our journeys to becoming and receiving all that He has stored up for us.

These three strategies—1) Study the Scriptures; 2) Verbally Declare the Scriptures; and 3) Record and Rehearse Personal Prophetic Promises—when purposefully applied, can definitely support you in your efforts to recover your mind, retrain your thoughts, and receive your promises. If you feel that you are actively doing all that you can in all three of these areas and still not receiving breakthrough, it may be possible that you are dealing with internal resignations. For such, it's important that you nullify any agreement you have made with the enemy, without knowledge, to retreat from your purpose. Take a moment to revisit the Personal Battleground section in Chapter 2 for a quick reminder on what this means.

PRAYER AND CONFESSION

Father, in the name of Jesus,

I humble myself in Your amazing presence. I thank You for Your goodness and Your love. You are consistent and an ever-present help in the time of trouble. You are the Lord of my mind and I decree that I have a sound mind. I apply the blood of Jesus on my mind and place upon myself the helmet of salvation. I thank You that I am covered. Every enemy that has come to steal my peace must go, in the name of Jesus! I command all spirits of torment, mental confusion, forgetfulness, mind control, mental illness, double-mindedness, fantasy, pain, pride, and memory recall to come out of my mind in the name of Jesus.

I break all curses of schizophrenia and command all spirits of double-mindedness, rejection, rebellion, and the root of bitterness to come out in the name of Jesus. I take authority over every spirit that comes to cause mental instability and I decree that Satan's plan has been stopped and that Your plans are being reinforced in the name of Jesus. I decree and declare that all plans set in motion by hell to drive me into an insane asylum are being diverted and I reverse those plans and I send that same confusion into the enemies' camp, in Jesus' name! I have a sound mind; my thoughts are pure; my mind is focused on Jesus; I think on things that bring life and peace! Father, release angels that come to bring breakthrough and supernatural strength to come to my defense today, in Jesus' name!

I decree and declare that I will not breakdown, I will break through!

ENDNOTE

1. Caroline Leaf, *Think, Learn, Succeed: Understanding and Using Your Mind to Thrive at School, the Workplace, and Life* (Grand Rapids, MI: Baker Books, 2018).

CHAPTER 5

▮▯▮▯▮▯

How the Enemy Sees Us Versus How God Sees Us

How satan Sees Us

When we understand that God sees us completely different from the way we see ourselves and the way our enemy sees us, it's much harder for the enemy to torment us mentally. It's so easy for us to view ourselves through lenses of hurt, past pains, betrayals, rejection, and all types of things that life introduces us to and lays on our shoulders. When we look at ourselves this way, we cannot truly embrace the truths of the

Word of God and we can't effectively rebuke the devil who comes to plant even uglier thoughts in us.

The reality is that the enemy is jealous of us and wants to destroy us so that we will miss out on the very thing that he lost eternally when he was kicked out of heaven. But I don't want to focus on the negative ways the enemy sees us, what I want to highlight specifically is that he sees sometimes what we do not, and what he sees sometimes works for us and not against us. For instance, let's look at Daniel:

> *And commanded some of the strongest soldiers in his army to tie up Shadrach, Meshach and Abednego and throw them into the blazing furnace. So these men, wearing their robes, trousers, turbans and other clothes, were bound and thrown into the blazing furnace. The king's command was so urgent and the furnace so hot that the flames of the fire killed the soldiers who took up Shadrach, Meshach and Abednego, and these three men, firmly tied, fell into the blazing furnace. Then King Nebuchadnezzar leaped to his feet in amazement and asked his advisers, "Weren't there three men that we tied up and threw into the fire?" They replied, "Certainly, Your Majesty." He said, "Look! I see four men walking around in the fire, unbound and unharmed, and the fourth looks like a son of the gods" (Daniel 3:20-25).*

What stands out to me so powerfully in this passage of Scripture is that it doesn't say these three men who were tossed in that fire saw the fourth man in there with them. It says that Nebuchadnezzar, their opposer, the one who was seeking to kill them, is the one who had eyes to see the fourth man in the fire—actively shielding the three from consumption. I love that, because what it says to me is that when the enemy looks in our direction, he is able to see our Helper! He is not blind to the fact that we don't have to fight him on our own or in our own strength. He can see, even when we can't, that we are not alone and that the One who favors us steps onto every battleground with us to fight for us, isn't that powerful?

When Satan looks at us, he's able to see the Holy One who covers and shields us from his snares and sly sneak attacks. This doesn't mean that he's not going to look for ways to get to us, but what it does mean is that our Helper is ever-present and ready to show up when the enemy is looking to destroy us. I want you to keep that in mind every time you find yourself in the fires of life. Because you are not alone, those fires simply cannot consume you. The same was true for Job:

> *"Does Job fear God for nothing?" Satan replied. "Have you not put a hedge around him and his household and everything he has? You have blessed the work of his hands, so that his flocks and herds are spread throughout the land. But now stretch out your hand and strike everything he has, and he will surely curse you to your face"* (Job 1:9-11).

When God approached Satan about Job, he couldn't say anything but the obvious. What was obvious for him was that God placed a hedge around him, his household, and all that belonged to him, and everything he owned and looked after was blessed. He pointed out what God already knew, but what I particularly love is that he himself knew and couldn't deny the evidence that God favored Job and was intentional about the way He cared for him.

The same is true for us. When Satan walks the earth looking for his next prey, the reason he looks in our direction is because he can see that we are favored and loved by the God of heaven and earth. Job was volunteered, literally introduced to Satan to be tried because of the way He walked before the Lord. What we can pull from this is not just the enemy's pursuit of us at God's suggestion, but the idea that he is very aware of who we are and what we carry. In those moments when we find ourselves questioning whether or not we are covered, favored, blessed, or the list can go on and on, the truth of the matter is that our greatest enemy can plainly see what we sometimes forget. Remember this!

How God Sees Us

God loves us enough to cover us. It's only through His eyes that we can we find our true identity. Knowing what He thinks about us is so important when it comes to our willingness to trust Him! Until you know how He feels about you, how can you believe or embrace His promises for you? It's difficult to receive His words and His blessings when you are not convinced that He sees you positively.

Psalm 139:13-18 (MSG) says:

Oh yes, you shaped me first inside, then out;
You formed in my mother's womb.
I thank you, High God—you're breathtaking!
Body and soul, I am marvelously made!
I worship in adoration—what a creation!
You know me inside and out,
You know every bone in my body;
You know exactly how I was made, bit by bit,
How I was sculpted from nothing into
something.
Like an open book, you watched me grow from
conception to birth;
All the stages of my life were spread out before
you,
The days of my life all prepared before I'd even
lived one day.
Your thoughts—how rare, how beautiful!
God, I'll never comprehend them!
I couldn't even begin to count them—
Any more than I could count the sand of the
sea.
Oh, let me rise in the morning and live always
with you!

Reads like poetry, doesn't it? God loves you so much that He literally put every part of you together with His own hands! Think about that for a bit. When we go to work, no matter where it is, your boss has assistants and the assistants have assistants. There's always someone pushing things off for others to do; in some cases it's because the task is beneath them, in others it's simply because they don't have time, but

I'm sure you see where I'm going with this. It's amazing that of the billions of people on the planet, God uniquely and tailor-made every one of them! He didn't get bored or too tired and pass you off to His assistant. He didn't hire someone else to do the rest of His job for Him. He's still designing and sculpting human beings to this day! How's that for adjusting the way you think He sees you? He knows you through and through!

God also loves you enough to think of you often. Jeremiah 29:11 (KJV) tells us, *"For I know the thoughts that I think toward you, saith the Lord, thoughts of peace, and not of evil, to give you an expected end."* Not only is He the God of the entire universe, but He has you and me on His mind! I don't know about you, but it doesn't matter how long I've been in relationship with Him or how many people I am able to share the gospel with, this thought will always amaze me and put things into proper perspective. God thinks of me and has planned my life day by day, to get me to the end He wrote out for me.

Psalm 40:5 (NLT) says, *"O Lord my God, you have performed many wonders for us. Your plans for us are too numerous to list. You have no equal. If I tried to recite all your wonderful deeds, I would never come to the end of them."* He still performs wonders, *for us!* He who is without equal thinks enough of us to still work wonders, to still make plans for us, how incredible is that? How many CEOs of corporations can you think of who know each employee of their company by name? Or even by position?

God delights in you. Psalm 147:11 says, *"The Lord delights in those who fear him, who put their hope in his unfailing love."*

To delight means to find great pleasure in, to charm and captivate. This verse says that God is completely captivated by you, His creation, as long as you find your hope in Him.

PRAYER AND CONFESSION

Father, in Jesus' name,

I see myself the way You see me and I make these statements my daily confession:

I am the righteousness of God.

I am the head and not the tail.

My head never lacks fresh oil.

I am crowned with glory.

I walk in new mercies.

I live in the grace of God and it's limitless.

God will always love me and there is nothing I can do to earn it.

God is not angry with me.

I am never beyond repair.

His thoughts are good toward me.

He will always be with me.

He's a good, kind, and loving Father.

He is not like a human being, He's perfect.

He's never changing.

I thank You, Lord, that according to Your Word, Your plans for me are good and Your thoughts toward me are endless. I have been handcrafted by You and made in Your image, therefore I am wonderfully made. I can't thank You enough for loving me with an everlasting love. I am highly favored because You are my Father. You love me enough to call me Your very own son/daughter, for that I am eternally grateful. Help me to daily put on new lenses to see myself the way You see me. I bind the hand of the enemy who comes to distort the way I see You and subsequently, the way I see myself. Daily I will strive to put on the mind of Christ to honor, love, and serve You for Your boundless love and grace toward me. In Jesus' name.

BATTLEGROUND NUMBER 2

WINNING THE WAR IN THE FLESH

CHAPTER 6

TACKLING THE FLESH

LET'S BE HONEST, THE LIFESTYLE OF A BELIEVER doesn't always look appealing or easy, to say the very least. The reason it doesn't look appealing or easy is directly related to our fleshly desires that are always in complete opposition to the will of God for our lives. Pleasing God only looks difficult to a believer who hasn't learned to put their flesh under subjection by submitting themselves wholly to the Lord. When you have a desire to please God, although your flesh will put up a great fight, it will not win once you have decided to walk in the spirit.

Tackling the flesh is essential for every believer and we don't need any other reason to want to do so other than knowing that the flesh directly opposes God! Over the next few pages we will target distinct ways to tackle our flesh so it cannot rob of us of the great joy of fulfilling our purpose on earth.

The flesh is selfish and quite creative. It's "me, me, me" attitude is what boldly shows up to suffocate the life out of our willingness to be led of the Holy Spirit. Whenever we should be doing one thing, it will always come up with a better suggestion for something so much more appealing for us to be doing in that moment. When we feel God pulling us into prayer or to study the Word, our flesh suggests that we should find something to eat or watch a movie.

When our spirit is longing to be found in heartfelt worship, our flesh would much rather call up a good friend and have a conversation about absolute nothingness just to pass the time. When we know that it's time for another fast, our flesh tells us that it's not necessary and to put it off for another week or two. No matter what godly instance, our flesh will always have a better suggestion. It really depends on which one we feed the most—be it our flesh or our spirit—that determines our adherence to God's plan. Romans 6:20-21 from The Message Bible says:

> *As long as you did what you felt like doing, ignoring God, you didn't have to bother with right thinking or right living, or right anything for that matter. But do you call that a free life? What did you get out of it? Nothing you're proud of now. Where did it get you? A dead end.*

See, yielding to the flesh is literally the act of ignoring God. When His promptings are met with disobedience because we'd prefer to do other things, what we are actually doing is telling Him that He isn't in control and we don't want Him in control. When He's not in control, we think we are; however, the enemy of our souls is actively controlling our thoughts, feelings, and actions, leading us to that dead end Paul wrote about.

Romans 8:7-8 (AMP) tells us, *"the mind of the flesh [with its sinful pursuits] is actively hostile to God. It does not submit itself to God's law, since it cannot, and those who are in the flesh [living a life that caters to sinful appetites and impulses] cannot please God."* I know that's a lot to digest. What this says to me is, first, the flesh has a mind of its own and boldly stands against God. Second, it cannot submit to God; and last, it cannot please God! For these reasons, it's absolutely vital that we get our flesh under control. With our flesh in control, there's no way we can win the battle against the kingdom of darkness. This makes sense because when the flesh is in control, God is not.

The flesh is enmity (directly opposing) toward God, which means in any battle, when our flesh is not subdued, we're on the wrong side of the battleground! Not only is our flesh the source of our weakness but it is also, within us, God's enemy. It has the potential and power to keep us from our destiny as long as we allow it to rule our lives and make our decisions for us. Here's a simple truth: we haven't made Him Lord if we're still giving in to our fleshly desires and allowing those desires to have the final say in our lives. Galatians 5:19-21 (KJV) tells us:

*Now the works of the flesh are manifest, which
are these; adultery, fornication, uncleanness,
lasciviousness, idolatry, witchcraft, hatred,
variance, emulations, wrath, strife, seditions,
heresies, envyings, murders, drunkenness,
revellings, and such like: of the which I tell
you before, as I have also told you in time past,
that they which do such things shall not inherit
the kingdom of God.*

The Living Bible Translation puts it this way:

*But when you follow your own **wrong inclinations,** your lives will produce these evil results:
impure thoughts, eagerness for lustful pleasure, idolatry, spiritism (that is, encouraging
the activity of demons), hatred and fighting,
jealousy and anger, constant effort to get the
best for yourself, complaints and criticisms,
the feeling that everyone else is wrong except
those in your own little group—and there will
be wrong doctrine, envy, murder, drunkenness, wild parties, and all that sort of thing.
Let me tell you again, as I have before, that
anyone living that sort of life will not inherit
the Kingdom of God.*

Romans 8:6 (AMP) says:

*Now **the mind of the flesh is death** [both
now and forever—because it pursues sin]; but
the mind of the Spirit is life and peace [the*

spiritual well-being that comes from walking with God—both now and forever].

I like to refer to the flesh as the "womb of sin." As this verse from Romans 8 explains, the mind of the flesh pursues sin and sin only. The more you give in to it, the more those impulses and desires multiply and give birth to more and more of its kind, which eventually brings forth death. Not only does the flesh rob you of your ability to please God, but it also robs you of the peace He promised to you as a believer and the full life you are purposed and designed to live.

The main focus of this chapter is not to just highlight sin, but to give you a clear understanding of what you can do to win in your personal war against your flesh and to honor God with the fruit your life produces. Yes, we were all born in sin and shaped in iniquity (Psalm 51:5); however, we were offered a new life in Christ when we were born again. Ephesians 2:1-10 (NLT) tells us:

Once you were dead because of your disobedience and your many sins. You used to live in sin, just like the rest of the world, obeying the devil—the commander of the powers in the unseen world. He is the spirit at work in the hearts of those who refuse to obey God. All of us used to live that way, following the passionate desires and inclinations of our sinful nature. By our very nature we were subject to God's anger, just like everyone else.

But God is so rich in mercy, and he loved us so much, that even though we were dead because of our sins, he gave us life when he raised Christ from the dead. (It is only by God's grace that you have been saved!) For he raised us from the dead along with Christ and seated us with him the heavenly realms because we are united with Christ Jesus. So God can point to us in all future ages as examples of the incredible wealth of his grace and kindness toward us, as shown in all he has done for us who are united with Christ Jesus.

God saved you by his grace *when you believed. And you can't take credit for this; it is a gift from God. Salvation is not a reward for the good things we have done, so none of us can boast about it. For we are God's masterpiece. He has created us anew in Christ Jesus, so we can do the good things he planned for us long ago.*

Grace literally pulled us from the death we were wrapped in as a result of sin and gave us a whole new life, not because we deserve it, but because He loved us enough! Now it is up to us to love Him enough to want to please Him with the lives He has entrusted to us by killing the flesh and not being led and controlled by it any longer. The question is, can we love Him the way He loved us? He loved us enough to die; now, are we willing to love Him so much that we can surrender to death as well? To the death of everything in us that does not glorify Him?

The truth is, if we don't kill this flesh, it will surely kill us—that is its purpose! Christ was the ultimate sacrifice. He died physically so that we could live spiritually and have a relationship with our Father—who can't stand to look at our flesh. The only thing that keeps us from that relationship He gave His life for is our flesh, full of sinful demands and endless expectations.

Let's talk about how to kill it.

Sin is defined as simply missing the mark. According to Romans 3:23, we are all guilty, not one person is exempt, other than Christ Himself. The only way to break the cycles of sin our flesh creates is to do as Galatians 5:16 tells us, *"So I say, walk by the Spirit, and you will not gratify the desires of the flesh."* In order for us to walk in the Spirit, we must first receive the Spirit. The Holy Spirit enables us to think and align ourselves with the Word of God and the will of God. Without the Holy Spirit, it is impossible for us to gain the victory over our flesh. Scripture refers to the Holy Spirit as a "helper" and as our "guide." With Him in us, pleasing God becomes so much easier.

CHAPTER 7

THE BATTLEGROUND OF PURPOSE

Now Jesus, full of the Holy Spirit, left the Jordan and was led by the Spirit into the wild. For forty wilderness days and nights he was tested by the Devil. He ate nothing during those days, and when the time was up he was hungry.

The Devil, playing on his hunger, gave the first test: "Since you're God's Son, command this stone to turn into a loaf of bread."

Jesus answered by quoting Deuteronomy: "It takes more than bread to really live."

For the second test he led him up and spread out all the kingdoms of the earth on display at once. Then the Devil said, "They're yours in all their splendor to serve your pleasure. I'm in charge of them all and can turn them over to whomever I wish. Worship me and they're yours, the whole works."

Jesus refused, again backing his refusal with Deuteronomy: "Worship the Lord your God and only the Lord your God. Serve him with absolute single-heartedness."

For the third test the Devil took him to Jerusalem and put him on top of the Temple. He said, "If you are God's Son, jump. It's written, isn't it, that 'he has placed you in the care of angels to protect you; they will catch you; you won't so much as stub your toe on a stone'?"

"Yes," said Jesus, "and it's also written, 'Don't you dare tempt the Lord your God.'"

That completed the testing. The Devil retreated temporarily, lying in wait for another opportunity (Luke 4:1-13 MSG).

I know what you're thinking, this Scripture passage is so meaty! The fact is, we all go through seasons of great testing, and a lot of times, we don't even know to call it that. The enemy puts many of his efforts into trying to convince us out of the will of God by promising us things he can never actually give us. The Bible tells us that the earth and the fullness thereof belongs to God (Psalm 24:1-3), so how can Satan promise to give us anything that isn't his?

Well, the truth is, as long as we're earthbound, he can make these things look so appealing until we are willing to sell out just to have a little piece of it, *temporarily!* So many believers give up their eternal peace for something that the enemy can only satisfy us with for a moment, isn't that something?

In this story from Luke 4, we see Jesus being tested not once, not twice, but three times. The enemy was set on giving everything he had to get Jesus to walk away from His purpose for being here by lies and deception. There's so much we can learn from Jesus' deportment and His response to the enemy.

First, Jesus had just completed a fast. This tells us that when you've surrendered your flesh to God during a season of fasting and prayer, the enemy will lie in wait to make a grand entrance as soon as you come out. For him, he thinks that you are at your most vulnerable and your weakest point because you're empty. What he doesn't understand is that although you may be physically empty, you are spiritually full! Jesus was not only able to look Satan in the face and shoot him with the Scripture again and again, but Jesus did it with poise and great strength.

That brings me to my next point: Jesus did not try to argue with the enemy using His own thoughts, wits, or charm. Jesus used what was already written! It's important that we learn the art of shutting down the enemy of our soul with the Word of God, which was written for that very purpose! Hebrews 4:12 tells us, *"For the word of God is alive and active. Sharper than any double-edge sword, it penetrates even to dividing soul and spirit, joints and marrow; it judges the thoughts and attitudes of the heart."*

The Word of God has the power to cut off Satan's very next sentence and cause him to have to rethink his next move against you. We cannot defeat him without the Word of God. Remember, he can quote the Scriptures (deceptively) and he knows fully who you are; if you fail to use the Word of God, your most powerful resource, you will fail every test he sends in your direction. Don't try to whip the devil with your words without them being seasoned with the Scriptures!

Next, the enemy will try to get us to worship him. Many think that if they're not actually bowing down physically, they're not worshiping him. But the truth is, as long as we live according to our fleshly desires and feeding that appetite, we are bowing to something other than our God. This is important to understand. It's not always that God doesn't want us to have great things, however, when they have the ability to change our heart toward Him, that's when He will purposely and intentionally keep them from us. This test reveals what we value, those things we secretly desire! This test was designed to expose whether or not Jesus' desires for things outweighed His desire to please God and complete His assignment on earth. If Satan offered you the world, would you take it?

If you have to wonder or take time to think about that, you, my dear, are in danger of failing one of the greatest tests of your life. Our hearts are exposed when we are offered the things we want so much that we are willing to "crucify Him afresh" to get them (see Hebrews 6:6). Examining and evaluating your heart and your desires at various times is always a powerful tool and will help you to pass this test—as it will come repeatedly.

PRAYER AND CONFESSION

Father, in the name of Jesus, I give Your name the glory, honor, and praise! Your love for me is better than life and Your goodness can never be earned but is given generously. I thank You that You have set me free and that You are unlocking new dimensions of my calling and destiny. I understand that Satan has come to steal, kill, and destroy, but You have come that I might have abundant life. Let that same anointing that rested on Jesus in the wilderness rest on me, in Jesus' name! I am more than a conqueror, being transformed in His image, and flesh will no longer have dominion over me. I am a child of God.

My purpose will be fulfilled; I break all spirits of distraction and confusion. All spirits that come to misdirect and thwart Your original purpose for my life is bound in Jesus' name! The devil is a liar and I stand in the truth of Your Word.

I break the power of all generational sin, knowing and unknowing. I ask You to forgive and cleanse me from all unrighteousness, in the name of Jesus! Satan, you are a liar and I will not live in your trap any longer. Jesus, I repent on behalf of my entire bloodline. I ask that all patterns of sin in my life be destroyed, in Jesus' name. I will win the war over the flesh and live in victory. I will live holy because You are holy! Thank You, God, for watching over me and ensuring that Your plans for me are completed, in Jesus' name.

BATTLEGROUND NUMBER 3

WINNING THE WAR
IN THE SPIRIT

CHAPTER 8

Exposing Hell's Agenda

Now that we have dealt with both the mind and the flesh, it's time to dive into the spirit. I wanted to tackle this last, not because it ranks last, but because there are some things that need to be dealt with first if we're going to effectively utilize our weapons in the spirit realm.

Before we can successfully dismantle anything in the spirit, it's vitally important that we get our minds and our flesh under control; because if not, we are bound to lose every battle in the spirit. Our opponent is no dummy. When we have not dealt with strongholds in our minds and flesh, he has all that he needs to keep us tangled and tied up—and defeated when it comes to anything in the spirit.

If you made it this far, I do not doubt how serious you are about winning in warfare! With the tools given so far and the ones you're about to receive, well, let's just say hell is angry!

The spirit realm is the battleground where heaven and hell are at war around the clock for the souls of every human being. Angels and demons are at work at all times; and unlike natural wars, they don't get tired or give up in the middle of a battle. They have been employed and given a job with fully defined roles, both to lead you to the masters they serve. Angels, of course, are assigned to provide assistance to you in an effort to usher you to the Father in heaven; while demons are sent to ensnare you and usher you to the grips of Satan and ultimately his fiery abode, hell.

One of the main and major spiritual battles we will discuss in great detail is the spirit of fear. Others include the spirits of divination, witchcraft-Jezebel, sorcery, and more. We must know how these spirits gain access to us and what we can do to be delivered from them. Second Corinthians 10:2-4 says:

> *I beg you that when I come I may not have to be as bold as I expect to be toward some people who think that we live by the standards of this world. For though we live in the world, we do not wage war as the world does. The weapons we fight with are not the weapons of the world. On the contrary, **they have divine power to demolish strongholds.***

Not only does this Scripture passage let us know that we have been given the weapons we need to wage a good warfare, but also that one of the purposes of our weapons is to demolish strongholds. This opens our eyes to the reality that strongholds are weapons, instruments designed by hell to destroy us—but God's plan is to demolish them, *through us!*

Before we go any further, I want to first define strongholds and legal rights as understanding these are a prerequisite for successfully engaging in spiritual warfare.

WHAT ARE STRONGHOLDS?

Strongholds are incorrect thinking patterns that we, knowingly and sometimes unknowingly, embrace and allow to become part of our natural thinking processes. They are not usually formed overnight, but are built over time. These thinking patterns are introduced to us both before and after receiving salvation. They are created by systematic lies not just fed to us, but lies that we believed. These lies team up together and become building blocks that construct literal fortresses in our minds that keep the truth from entering and the lies from exiting.

Some of these patterns are embedded in us from our childhood, others inherited or passed on to us from our parents and other influential people in our lives, and others are embraced via good and bad experiences, whether at our own hands or at the hands of others. These patterns affect our feelings, our perceptions, and our responses to everything we deal with in life. Because they are incorrect, they have a great deal of influence on our overall spiritual health as they are fortresses constructed and designed to keep us from ever obtaining true freedom.

The very next verse in the Scripture referenced, Second Corinthians 10:5 says, *"We demolish arguments and every pretension that sets itself up against the knowledge of God, and we take captive every thought to make it obedient to Christ."* These strongholds are set up within us with a distinct purpose—to keep us from receiving, believing, and understanding the things of God. So you can imagine that even for those of us who are strong in our faith, when we still have strongholds living in our minds, we can never tap into the fullness of who God is or what He desires for us. With active strongholds within us, we can never uncover our full potential and become the epitome of who God created us to be.

> ## WITH ACTIVE STRONGHOLDS WITHIN US, WE CAN NEVER UNCOVER OUR FULL POTENTIAL AND BECOME THE EPITOME OF WHO GOD CREATED US TO BE.

These strongholds create a wall between us and the Father, keeping Him from having total access to us. Demons work through these strongholds to keep us enslaved and in bondage, seemingly unable to break free. Since they are built on lies and deception, the only way to tear them down is with the truth—and the only truth demons and strongholds recognize is the Word of God.

Because we know that God is all-powerful, we understand that if He wants to, He can easily knock down the walls to get to us. However, because He has given us free will, He leaves some parts of our freedom totally up to us. When we desire absolute freedom, we must make a personal decision to agree with and partner with God for our deliverance. With this commitment, we are able to renounce these strongholds and break their power by adhering to the Scriptures and driving out the demons that are working through them in Jesus' name.

Since strongholds are formed in the mind and dwell there, it's important that our minds are renewed. Romans 12:2 tells us:

> Do not conform to the pattern of this world, but be transformed by the renewing of your mind. Then you will be able to test and approve what God's will is—his good, pleasing and perfect will.

It is only once our minds are renewed that we are able to understand the will of God for our lives, which includes His desire for us to walk in His power and demolish strongholds. Strongholds are weapons of hell against us, but when we are in Christ, we ourselves become weapons against them! The following are seven strategies for breaking strongholds and maintaining your freedom from them:

1. **Daily Decree**: "No outside force will think through me!"

Philippians 2:5 (NKJV) says, *"Let this mind be in you which was also in Christ Jesus."*

2. **Take Authority!** Once you come out of agreement with it, it must exit. When these demons try to return, stand firm against them declaring the Word of God.

    Ephesians 6:12-17 says:

    *For our struggle is not against flesh and blood, but against the rulers, against the authorities, against the powers of this dark world and against the spiritual forces of evil in the heavenly realms. Therefore put on the full armor of God, so that when the day of evil comes, you may be able to **stand your ground**, and after you have done everything, to stand. Stand firm then, with the belt of truth buckled around your waist, with the breastplate of righteousness in place, and with your feet fitted with the readiness that comes from the from the gospel of peace. In addition to all this, take up the shield of faith, with which you can extinguish all the flaming arrows of the evil one. Take the helmet of salvation and the sword of the Spirit, which is the word of God.*

3. **Think About What You Are Thinking About.** Yes, you read that right! It's important that you track your thoughts and are ever mindful to assess where they are taking you. When you do

this, you are able to direct and redirect them as necessary.

Proverbs 23:7 (NKJV) tells us, *"For as he thinks in his heart, so is he...."*

4. **Write a Plan or Strategy Specific for Every Battle You Are Facing.** We talked about being prepared for battle in a previous chapter. When soldiers are readying themselves for war, they take the time to devise a plan. This enables them to put necessary strategies in place beforehand, giving them calculative tools easily accessible during the battle. Not only does this give them extra confidence, it also weakens their opponent's. Scripture says write it down and make it plain so that whoever reads it may run—sometimes that person who reads it and runs into battle has to be *you!*

Habakkuk 2:2 (NKJV) instructs us, *"Then the Lord answered me and said: 'Write the vision and make it plain on tablets, that he may run who reads it.'"*

5. **Journal Your Victories!** You'd be surprised how encouraging this is! Much like rehearsing the recorded prophetic promises of God in times of weakness, being able to remind yourself of previous victories has such an empowering effect on your mind and spirit. When you

revisit past victories, you don't just remember your win, you'll also remember what it felt like in those moments when you thought you wouldn't win. When you are reminded, that memory has the ability to sustain you amid your next battle, giving you added strength and incentive to fight the good fight! If we don't record it, it could be lost, because it's so easy to forget those wins when we are experiencing moments when we feel like we're going to lose.

Psalm 78:7 (NKJV) reveals to us, *"That they might set their hope in God, **and not forget the works of God,** but keep His commandments."*

Revelation 1:19 says, *"Write, therefore, what you have seen, what is now and what will take place later."*

6. **Defend Yourself Out Loud!** Remember, your words have creative power. They must be spoken in order to take form. Decree strength, peace, sweet rest—whatever you need before, during, and after any battle!

Psalm 118:17 (NKJV) tells us, *"I shall not die, but live, and declare the works of the Lord."*

7. **Choose to Not Give Up!** However often you need to do this, do it!

Second Chronicles 15:7 says, *"But as for you, be strong and do not give up, for your work will be rewarded."*

Galatians 6:9 says, *"Let us not become weary in doing good, for at the proper time we will reap a harvest if we do not give up."*

Hebrews 12:1-3 says:

Therefore, since we are surrounded by such a great cloud of witnesses, let us throw off everything that hinders and the sin that so easily entangles. And let us run with perseverance the race marked out for us, fixing our eyes on Jesus, the pioneer and perfecter of faith. For the joy set before him he endured the cross, scorning its shame, and sat down at the right hand of the throne of God. Consider him who endured such opposition from sinners, so that you will grow weary and lose heart.

A BRIEFING ON LEGAL RIGHTS

A legal right is the thing that gives demons permission to hold us captive and to harass us. Whenever or if ever a person is bound by a demonic spirit, it is important for you to understand that that spirit has a legal right. Hell has to follow the protocols that God has set in place just as we do. Legal rights are granted through the ancestral line, also known as generational curses, or granted by us via sin. When we sin, we not only engage with and entertain demonic spirits, but we open doors of access for demons to walk right in.

Before a deliverance minister can get to the root of what has people bound and free them, they must first locate the points of access. It is only once the legal right is broken that all of the accompaniments can be removed. This is made available for every believer, not a select few.

Now we are ready to break strongholds and dismantle satanic agendas! It's time for you to arrest what has been arresting you.

CHAPTER 9

THE SPIRIT OF FEAR

BEFORE WE CAN EFFECTIVELY AND VICTORIOUSLY wage war in the spirit, we must first tackle and dismantle the spirit of fear. We all experience it, no one is exempt. It's an emotion created by an inner belief that a person, thing, situation, or occurrence is *likely* to harm us in some way. As we anticipate the outcomes of circumstances, we find ourselves tormented, anxious, and dreading the seemingly endless—mostly imagined—possibilities. You cannot battle a demon that you do not recognize, so I want you to see fear for what it really is. In addition, you will be made aware of the prophetic signs that uncertainty has found a resting place in your life—and realize that when those signs show up, fear shows up in very specific ways.

How does fear manifest? There are so many ways that the spirit of fear creeps in, many of which we will discuss in the following pages. Fear shows up in a variety of ways and are different for all of us. I understand fear intimately. I was bound to the spirit as a child, and for more than twenty years of my life, I battled almost every kind of fear that you can imagine—I know firsthand how fear can operate in a person's life and that its intent is to destroy. Yes, I understand how fear can suppress you, but I also understand how you can overcome it.

It's important to understand that fear is never something that just simply shows up on our doorstep—it always walks through an open door. For me, that door was left wide open by the gaping hole in my heart that my alcohol- and drug-addicted father who left me behind created. It was left open by the physical abandonment and abuse that I endured. It was left open by the curse of mental illness on my family, a curse that could be readily traced back for multiple generations. I witnessed this firsthand at the hands of my mother who herself suffered much abuse and lived her entire life marred by the remnants of trauma.

As a little girl, I remember being afraid of *everything*. I was afraid of the dark, afraid of closets, afraid of bridges, you name it and chances are I was afraid of it. Being the child I was, I attributed these fears to scary stories I'd heard about monsters and ghosts that I'd never seen. Soon though, it would be revealed to me as I journeyed, sometimes stumbled down my path to womanhood, that the spirit of fear that gripped me and held me hostage was about far more than some imaginary beings that went *thump* in the night.

Oftentimes, people who are bound by the spirit of fear are those who have dynamic, tremendous, outrageous calls on their lives, but fear keeps them from ever fully embracing and honoring that call. Those who are bound by the spirit of fear may never preach or teach, they may never bring their God-given idea(s) to fruition, they may never build the church, school, or company as long as this spirit is taking up residence within them. Fear is bondage and it is demonic. It comes to prevent you from becoming who you really are as a son or daughter of God, so you must battle it with everything in you. As a Kingdom citizen—as a child of God—fear certainly could not keep me, and it won't keep you either!

Fear can be directly related to an orphan heart. An orphan heart is a heart that has not yet experienced the transforming love of God. An orphan heart is one that has not accepted the Father's love and has no idea what that love looks like. If you are suffering from an orphan heart like me, you may have lived through a very traumatic childhood. You may have been tormented and physically, emotionally, or sexually abused. You may have been harassed by demon spirits. These are events that allow fear to enter into our spirits; and if we never allow God to rescue us from that edge, we'll never escape fear's stronghold. Romans 8:14-17 says:

> *For those who are led by the Spirit of God are the children of God. The Spirit you received does not make you slaves, so that you **live in fear again**; rather, the Spirit you received brought about your adoption to sonship. And by him we cry, "Abba, Father." The Spirit himself testifies with our spirit that we are*

God's children. Now if we are children, then
we are heirs—heirs of God and co-heirs with
Christ, if indeed we share in his sufferings in
order that we may also share in his glory.

This Scripture ties the orphan heart with the spirit of fear, which shows us why deliverance is so necessary. When we've been abandoned, we must be delivered from that trauma and all of the insecurities that come with it. We must experience, firsthand, the delivering power of God so that our orphan hearts can be healed, once and for all. We must allow God to defeat that spirit of fear so that we never again fall prey to believing the enemy's lies.

Let's take a closer look at the anatomy of the spirit of fear:

- Fear usually starts with an *event*.

- The enemy feeds the mind with a *lie* based on that fear.

- We build a *defense* to protect ourselves from what we fear.

- We *respond* to the world according to what we believe to now be true.

Let's dig deeper.

THE EVENT

The cycle of fear typically starts with an event in our lives that drives us to question the truth. For many of us, it was a traumatic or painful childhood event. As a little girl, I was abandoned and left in the hands of people who did not really care about me. I had aunts and cousins who would lock me in closets. They would torment me and tell me that Satan was in the closet. Knowing I was terrified, they would turn off all the lights, lead me into a room, and then jump out and scare me. I constantly felt threatened and unsafe. Something that may seem playful and harmless to one person may haunt someone else.

As previously stated, fear does not simply just show up. More often than not, we can trace its entrance into our lives back to something significant that happened to us. Trauma opens us up to the spirit of fear, and fear is always birthed out of uncertainty. We are unsure if we will be protected or safe, so our natural response is to become afraid and to stop trusting, even after God assures us through His presence and His Word that we are safe with Him. Fear exists because there is something preventing you from trusting in God.

Maybe you were tormented or tortured in some way, too. Perhaps your event was triggered by something that someone said to you. Someone you loved and trusted may have dropped you, let you down, or your husband may have walked out on you. Somewhere, at some point in your life, you weren't sure if there would be someone there to protect you. And so fear found its way in, made a home, and never left.

Think about the person who is terrified to drive over a bridge. There is an uncertainty there. She is sitting in that car, afraid to death, asking herself if she will make it to the other side. There is no logical reason why she will not cross that bridge safely. There are no visible signs to make one even consider that the bridge will collapse. It is safe and sturdy.

There are plenty of other cars coming and going around her. But she would rather sit on the side of the road and wait for someone to drive her over it rather than go at it alone.

I know because I used to be her. I was afraid of crossing bridges. Before I sought deliverance from my fears, I would even go to the extremes of waiting at the edge of a bridge for an hour if I was driving alone because I did not want to take the challenge and drive across that bridge. My fear stemmed from a traumatic event in my childhood where my dad and I were crossing a bridge. The winds were so strong that I could feel the car trembling. Midway across, the hood of the car suddenly flew up. My father stopped the car and got out to close the hood. I was terrified. The enemy began flooding my head with lies that my dad was going to die on that bridge. He didn't, but the seed had already planted. From that point on, I associated bridges with death. I believed that if I got on a bridge, I would die.

To overcome, I had to start training my thoughts and saying things to myself such as, "My life is in the hand of God. God is my strength, and He's my source, He's my life." Whenever I was confronted with that fear, I put my trust and my hope in God. Had I not, I was consumed, reflecting on all the negative instead of the positive.

Being fearful of driving over a bridge is a natural example, but the same type of fear grips us in the spirit as well. Just like our physical destination is awaiting us on the other side of that bridge, our destiny awaits us on the other side of fear. Wherever fear is present, there is something on the other side that the enemy does not want you to understand or know about yourself. There is something on the other side that the enemy doesn't want you to know about your future. There is something great, something extraordinary that God has waiting for you on the other side—but you must break the bondage so that you can claim it. You must realize the truth that there is no spirit of fear or abandonment that can outmatch God. Once you accept that God is your Protector, your Father, and your Provider, all those fears that you are bound to will have no choice but to fall away.

THE LIE

The lie is like a seed that conceives and births what we believe to be truths in our minds. And like any other parasite, the lie feeds on something within us. It feeds on our fears, doubts, insecurities, etc. Fear is a vicious and relentless spirit that lies in wait, grappling for every opportunity to constrict us and keep us from walking into and experiencing the great things God has prepared for us. As such, it is indeed a spirit that we will have to confront repeatedly. It's gripped me in times past and I am certain that fear, in some capacity, has had a stronghold on you, too.

After any traumatic event occurs in our lives, the enemy knows that we are at our most vulnerable. Just like the opportunist he is, he jumps at the chance to speak the lie to our minds where it will take residence and will then replay over and over throughout our lives. Satan speaks it to us in first person, and because we are not listening with our spiritual ear in that moment, we confuse his voice with our own. We hear things like, *"God is not with me. If He was, this would have never happened to me."* We, being deceived, begin to believe what Satan says about our marriages, our failed relationships, disappointments by our pastors and other leaders. His lies initiate and launch a cycle of mistrust.

> ## THE TRUTH WILL ALWAYS SOUND LIKE THE WORD OF GOD.

This is why it is so important that we develop a strong sense of knowing and an ever-increasing ability to identify satanic voices and gestures that can so easily be mistaken for our own. How can you decipher the lie from the truth? Simple: the truth will always sound like the Word of God. The lie will sound like our own thoughts, our own imagination, and it rarely, if ever, aligns with the Word of God. Satan is a master manipulator! For this reason, it's imperative that we not just read, but study and learn the Word of God for ourselves. Let me share another intimate story about my battle with fear.

There was a time when I was afraid to die. The enemy fed me that lie almost all of my life; and while I was delivered from that lie and that spirit more than once (we will discuss the importance of deliverance later in this chapter) and I prayed it away whenever I was confronted with it, Satan would wait for an opportunity to attack my spirit with the fear of death whenever there was an open door for him to do so.

In 2016, I went into the hospital for surgery and that spirit was as strong as it had ever been. For days before my procedure, I grew more and more anxious. The lie of the enemy was loud and present in my mind telling me that he would kill me on the operating table, and I believed every word. I sought God. I prayed. I worshiped. I found myself in the midst of a battle for my sanity that I thought I'd won years ago, and Satan did everything he could to remind me that this war wasn't over.

On the morning of my procedure, I arrived at the hospital. As I lay on the table in the operating room waiting for the anesthesia to lull me into sleep, I was shaking and trembling so violently that I didn't know if I could close my eyes, even with the help of the strongest medication possible. However, amid my intense panic, somehow the peace of God managed to penetrate Satan's lies and threats that were successfully lodged in my mind, and I fell asleep. When I woke up a few hours later, I was fine and so relieved to be alive.

As I began to praise God, it was as if the enemy woke up too. He wasn't going down that easily. My body began experiencing some complications that the doctor hadn't prepared me for before the procedure. As the pain washed over me, I could hear the enemy taunting me. He assured me that I was on the verge of death. He guaranteed me that this was it—my ministry was over and coming to an end because I had dared to place an assault against the kingdom of darkness. I began to believe that he had power over me. Somewhere between being put to sleep and waking up in the recovery room, the lie had set in and took me captive. I went home a few days later in complete spiritual turmoil and breakdown. My body felt broken and so did my spirit. With the exception of my immediate family in my home, no one else had any idea what I was going through.

There I was, once again, facing that generational curse of mental illness. The spirit of fear was so strong that I knew I was staring another nervous breakdown directly in the face. The enemy's lies had attached themselves to my mind and my spirit, and I believed every untruth he whispered to me— until I remembered how to fight back!

I knew I needed to walk through the steps of deliverance. But first, I had to remember how to pray. I started praying in the spirit, and then I began declaring the truth over my own life. In no time, my faith began to increase. As I began to feel stronger, it was important for me to begin to change my spiritual atmosphere in a physical sense. I purposed to sit among the prophets in prophetic atmospheres of worship to absorb everything those environments had to offer me. Those spaces fed me with the Word of God and my spirit soaked it up, expanding my faith as if it were a sponge.

I began to surround myself with people who didn't hesitate to tell me the truth, individuals who knew the Word of God and would feed me the Scriptures. The Bible says, *"faith comes by hearing, and hearing by the word of God"* (Romans 10:17 NKJV), and so I knew that to be true. The more I heard the Word of God, the more my faith began to ignite and increase.

My friend, Prophetess Gabby, was like a secret weapon during that time. Times when I felt afraid, I would call her, and although I had not shared with her that I was in the grips of anxiety, she, being led by the Spirit of God, would begin flooding me with Scripture. Those Scriptures were like missiles and fiery darts against the enemy, literally disarming the darkness that was trying to arrest me in those moments. As I feasted on and filled myself with more and more of the Word of God, it demolished the strongholds that had formed in my life one by one; the prophetic words started coming. What God was doing was feeding me His truths to rid me of the lie that was trying to take root within me.

The enemy's lie, the fear of death, that stronghold in my life, fell away. Satan lost his grip on me. I was free! When I came to know Christ, I was no longer afraid of death. I fully understood that to be absent from the body was to be present with the Lord. I understood that I didn't have to be in bondage, I had a Father who loved me. I had to start thinking radically because my thoughts took me captive. I had to combat my fears of death in every way, including crossing bridges, by praying over myself. I had to encourage myself with this truth—if I die, I will open my eyes and be with the Lord. (See Second Corinthians 5:8.) So it was literally God's love and His Word that helped me to conquer those fears.

Now, I can cross any bridge. I can survive in the dark. I can walk through any door, any fire, to get to my destiny. The fear of death no longer has me ensnared. I was delivered from that demon. Deliverance is such a powerful weapon and it is vital for anyone who wants to completely break free from the stronghold of fear. I have personally gone through many deliverance sessions in my adult life, even in my time as a pastor and as a leader. I have gone through many sessions of deliverance because I recognized my need to be free if I was ever going to be a Moses to the people I am called to lead.

God did not give us the spirit of fear.

What we know for certain, according the Scriptures, is that God did not give us the spirit of fear (2 Timothy 1:7).

Instead, He gave us a threefold cord: power, love, and a sound mind to defeat fear. Whenever this cord is present and fully employed, there can be no fear. The stronghold takes root not solely because the lie exists, but because we believe it. If you are too afraid, too ashamed, or unwilling to be transparent enough to reach out and to admit that you need deliverance from a demon spirit, I encourage you, fight the urge to hide.

If you are unwilling to speak it or to ask for it, then you will never be set free. The minute you open your mouth and reach out for deliverance, God will send a deliverer your way, I promise you that. I am witness of that. If you are not in a house that offers deliverance, find one. Within a house of war and worship, you will find your freedom.

In the midst of the battle against the enemy's strongholds, we cannot forget that God is our Keeper. He is our Lord and He is on our side. He promises to never leave us or forsake us. God is always our Provider. It's important that you take time to study and get to know who God is as your Father and as your Provider. He is your Source, not people or anything around us. He clothes the lilies in the field, surely He will clothe and take care of us (Matthew 6:28). Because we are His sons and daughters and because of the promises He's made to us, we should fear nothing.

THE DEFENSE

Once we come into agreement with the lie in our hearts, we naturally start to build walls of defense, sometimes even unbeknown to us. We do this in an effort to keep ourselves from experiencing any more of the painful events and occurrences that opened the door for the lie in the first place. A defense is defined as the act of "resisting attack." Its purpose is to protect and guard against any attempts to hurt or ultimately destroy us.

In some scenarios, defenses are healthy. For example, it's needful and necessary for the armed forces of the United States to be well skilled in building impenetrable defenses so that terrorists are unable to break through and defeat us. However, when it comes to us as the children of God, our inner defenses can be much more harmful than they are helpful, and that's the enemy's plan. We tend to construct defenses that hinder our own mental, emotional, and sometimes even physical freedom. It may be a defense in our minds. We find ourselves harboring thoughts such as, "I will never allow anyone to hurt me like that again!" It may be a physical defense. We train ourselves to avoid any particular person or place that reminds us of our traumatic experiences and forces us to relive them.

These types of defenses allow us to create walls around our hearts and our spirits—some of which are so strong that no one can penetrate them, including God Himself. They prevent us from forgiving. They prevent us from receiving and experiencing complete healing from the pain of the traumatic event where the enemy planted the seed and erected the lie. However, it doesn't matter how hard we try to insulate ourselves trying to shield ourselves from further hurt, the spirit of fear still somehow manages to creep in. Our pain has a voice and it speaks to us.

Pain is one of the major tools the enemy of our souls looks to partner with in order to gain access to our spirit, distort our perceptions, and ultimately use our own hands to build the walls that keep us from ever truly fulfilling our purpose. So, plainly stated, you can run, but you cannot hide! These walls, built as a result of trauma and pain, need to be dealt with and torn down.

There is only one true way to push past your defenses, and that is to face your fears. I used to be sorely afraid of public speaking, but I was such a dramatic reader. My teachers would regularly choose me to read in class because I was so good at it. But one day, in the third grade, I got up and forgot my words and the entire auditorium laughed at me. After that event, the memory left an imprint, an unforgettable impression was forever etched in my mind, or so I thought. I lost sight of my gift and talent; none of it mattered anymore. The seed had been planted. Whenever I thought about reading in front of people, I'd be instantly consumed with the memory of all those children laughing at me and I'd immediately dismiss the idea. There was no way I was ever going to put myself through that kind of public humiliation again.

Fast forward to some years later, I was still traumatized. I had been called to preach what would be my very first sermon. The moment I stepped up to the podium, the enemy bombarded me with all of those memories—and before I knew it, I was that little third-grade girl all over again, forgetting my words and completely mortified as a crowd of people teased and made fun of me. At least, that's what I imagined was happening. Anytime I was invited to preach, I would literally shake like a leaf until one day I knew it was time for me to face it.

A few days later, I was sitting in front of Pastor Beverly Tucker, author of the *Setting the Captive Free* manual. She walked me through my entire childhood and all of the memory triggers, and before long, that event came to the surface. She called it out of me and while I was committed to dealing with the trauma, it did not immediately go away. My mind had to be reprogrammed. The seeds the enemy successfully planted in my mind and lodged in my memory had to be replaced with the Word of God and the things He said concerning me. This could only be done by consistently reading and studying His Word.

When I share that story, I am often asked how I was able to conquer the fear of public speaking and fully embrace who I was in the body of Christ. Aside from my work with Beverly, I started receiving major release through absorbing and digesting the Scriptures. I embraced the fullness of God through His Word, and in turn, I was able to fully embrace who I was. This didn't happen until I finally began to believe what the Word said about me. My mind needed to be renewed.

When you fill yourself with His Word, both through Scripture and through prophetic utterances, those walls of defense will begin to crumble. You'll no longer need to hide.

Not only were my thoughts reconditioned with the Word of God, they were also restructured through the power of the prophetic word. The prophetic word saved my life! Sometimes when you don't have the courage to do something that God is calling you to do, you need to get around people who can give you the language to define and bring clarity to where you are and where you're going. My spiritual father began to speak into my life and skillfully put language to who the Lord said I was and what I was called to be, called to do, and called to build.

Sometimes we just don't know how powerful we are or recognize in totality the call on our lives. God places prophets and prophetic people around us for such things. The prophetic word accompanied by the Word of God and prayer gave me the courage to be who God called me to be. Do I still get nervous? Yes. Do I still question my ability? At times, yes. I don't think that will ever go away. I believe that God sometimes uses those types of things to keep us humble and to keep us dependent upon Him. I understand that I cannot do anything for Christ outside of Him. Apart from Him, I'd die. My purpose would be over.

THE RESPONSE

Once the lie is at work through the defenses we've created, we respond to the world differently and the ways in which we perceive how people respond to us. Since our responses are based on a lie and our false, now-marred perceptions, they often trigger more painful events and we find ourselves in a perpetual cycle. It continues to repeat itself.

One of my daughters encountered an experience with abusive leadership at a church, and as a result, she feared leadership. She was deeply hurt, and it wounded her to the point that she became extremely controlling and refused to submit. To her, submission meant control and reminded her of the abuse she endured. Freeing her from that spirit of fear required great deliverance.

When she joined me at Kingdom Church International, now All Nations Worship Assemblies-Baltimore, I had to battle those emotional scars and spiritual battle wounds that she still carried from three years prior. I did everything I could to tear down those defensive walls that she'd built by attempting to show and teach her what healthy submission looked like. I exemplified for her, through myself and others, what respect and honor really look like, but in the beginning, she wasn't ready or able to receive any of it.

She'd made a contract, a covenant, within herself, which the enemy knew, that said, "I will never allow another person to do to me what they did to me." The spirit of Jezebel had set in and made her aggressive toward the leader God sent to walk her through her deliverance. She would attack me repeatedly, but it would be subtle and verbal. Her hurt and pain kept her stagnant for quite some time as she searched externally for the keys to her deliverance, which were actually within her own mind and spirit.

Finally, I'd had enough. "You will not make me pay for what your former leaders did," I told her one day after one of our regular verbal tussles about her behavior toward the other leaders within our church and toward me. Those words led to the breakthrough that I'd been praying for. For the first time, she was able to connect her fear to the pain from her past and to accept the responsibility for the role that she played in creating that fear. It was still a long road to her deliverance, but it had to begin with a step.

The spirit of fear will cause you to guard everything. With leadership, or anything or anyone else who has hurt you, you will set up a barricade as a means to protect yourself. The danger with barricades is that they are fortresses that keep the spirit of fear locked in and your deliverance locked out. Trust is what will combat the spirit of fear, not a response rooted in greater fear.

Every time you feel fear trying to come into your mind again, trust. Peter asked Jesus, *"Lord, how many times shall I forgive my brother or sister who sins against me? Up to seven times?' Jesus answered, 'I tell you, not seven times, but seventy-seven times'"* (Matthew 18:21-22). In other words, don't keep count. The spirit of fear will convince you not to forgive someone for the very thing that you need forgiveness for. Lack of trust in others and an inability to forgive keeps you from growing.

The enemy understands that leadership is necessary so he plants seeds of lies to ensure that we remain disconnected from our leaders. We have so many people who refuse to trust, and therefore submit, to their leaders which a large contributor to why our churches, our homes, and our nations are in such turmoil. Every house needs a leader. As sons and daughters, we must stop responding to our leaders from fear and hurt from our pasts, we must forgive.

The same woman who walked with me through my deliverance did the same for my daughter. Our experiences were so similar that it was freaky. It was during one of those sessions that I was reminded that my fear had traveled with me from my childhood through adulthood. What we refuse to be free from has a right to our children. When I refused to remain in bondage and enslaved, I not only freed myself, but by birthright I also freed my daughter.

FREEDOM COMES WHEN WE FACE OUR FEARS.

As believers, it is our responsibility to eat. What am I talking about, you ask? It is our responsibility to eat until we are full, until we are satisfied. However, you cannot be full until you are free, and you cannot be free until you are willing to be honest. Freedom comes when we face our fears. Freedom comes from the truths that are uncovered through transparency. Your transparency is the key to your deliverance. Be transparent with your leaders. Trust again. Trust and hope that God will bring you to your expected end. God never brings us to a place and allows us to experience anything that He is unwilling to bring you out, through, and to the other side of.

When the children of Israel were in bondage, God allowed them to experience many different things. He didn't bring despair or hurt to them, but He allowed it to be and He showed Himself strong and mighty before, during, and after it. God is ready and willing to do the same for you in your wilderness, but you have to allow your faith to rise. You have to understand that if God brought you through it, surely He will bring you out of it. It's time for you to believe and have hope in God again.

FEAR IS NOT A CONSEQUENCE.

Let me also remind you: fear is not a consequence. If you believe that you've done something so bad that your fears are a result of that behavior, I'm here to serve notice—that thought is a lie. Begin to dismantle the lie with this personalized truth in Second Timothy 1:7 (NKJV): *God has not given me the spirit of fear—He's given me power, love, and a sound mind.* I encourage you to stand on the Word of God. Start with Second Timothy 1:7, and as you begin to understand the power of the Scriptures, as I did when I began my deliverance journey, begin praying 1 John 4:18 also. Start praying the Scriptures over yourself daily. The transforming love of the Father and His Word will change the way you think. I promise! Here's one of my personal prayers you can start with:

PRAYER AND CONFESSION:

> *God, Your Word says there is no fear in love; You said perfect love casts out all fear. God, I pray that You would perfect Your love in me. Every area in me that has been planted because of hatred, bitterness, and all these other offenses, I pray, God, that You would uproot. Let me be delivered from the spirit of fear once and for all. I decree that fear has no power over me, because You are my God. Because You are my Father, I have no need to fear. Because You said you would never leave me in bondage to the spirit of fear. Amen.*

It is important for you to know that the battle with the spirit of fear is a consistent one. Once you defeat fear in one season, you can expect it to return in another. At every level of your success, there is fear to conquer and giants to slay. While you may not fear speaking in front of a crowd or becoming a leader, you may fear self-sabotage, which is rooted in rejection, or that God may change His mind and take something away from you that is already destined for you. Remember that the only person who can abort your destiny is you. God's intentions are sure. He's a consistent God.

There's also the fear of success and failure. When those fears stare you in the face and threaten to take you down, they serve as a reminder that, once again, you must come into agreement with who the Father fashioned and formed you to be. When you know that and you are secure in it, you realize that even if you fail, you can get up and try again as long as you're still breathing. If you succeed, you can thank God for it because it is His intention for you to win.

God wishes above all things that we would prosper—not just in the natural, but also in the spirit. Prosperity isn't just about money, but having a successful life. So come into agreement and be okay with who God has called you to be. Rise up and respond to fear as the man or woman of God that you are!

CHAPTER 10

Moving from Fear to Apostolic Authority

A S AN APOSTOLIC PEOPLE, WE MUST UNDERSTAND
that fear should never have dominion in our lives. We must destroy any opportunity that opens the door for the spirit of fear to enter. Demon spirits cannot hold you. Lack cannot hold you. Fear cannot hold you. You are a child of God. Proverbs 28:1 states: *"The wicked flee though no one pursues, but the righteous are as bold as a lion."* It's time for you to walk in your boldness.

Boldness is confidence. Boldness is fearlessness. Boldness is being unafraid to speak, to live, and to lead according to the Word of God. This is boldness and discipleship. This is who we are—His sons and daughters. As you move into this journey of boldness and courage, the following are a few Scriptures I'd you to read and study:

- Ephesians 3:12: *"In him and through faith in him we may approach God with freedom and confidence."*

- Philippians 1:20: *"I eagerly expect and hope that I will in no way be ashamed, but will have sufficient courage so that now as always Christ will be exalted in my body, whether by life or by death."*

- 1 Timothy 3:13: *"Those who have served well gain an excellent standing and great assurance in their faith in Christ Jesus."*

- 1 John 4:17: *"This is how love is made complete among us so that we will have confidence on the Day of Judgment: In this world we are like Jesus."*

- Acts 4:13: *"When they saw the courage of Peter and John and realized that they were unschooled, ordinary men, they were astonished and they took note that these men had been with Jesus."*

The definition of boldness—confidence, audaciousness, fearlessness—gives clear and concise language to who we *should* be and is undoubtedly prophetic of who we *will* be. It speaks to God's desire for us as His sons and daughters. He intends for us to be fearless and we receive this confidence, this boldness, in the name of Jesus Christ. God knows, and you should too, that boldness and courage are necessary qualifications for the work in the Kingdom to be completed. As apostolic women and men, we shouldn't be surprised that the enemy loves to inflict us with the spirit of fear.

First Peter 5:8 says, *"Be alert and of a sober mind. Your enemy the devil prowls around like a roaring lion looking for someone to devour."* This Scripture says that the enemy is like a lion. I want you to pay close attention to that. The enemy may have a roar, but so do we, the Spirit of the Lion of the tribe of Judah rests in us!

Second Timothy 1:7 (KJV) says: *"For God hath not given us the spirit of fear; but of power, and of love, and of a sound mind."*

Without boldness, power of love, and a sound mind, the enemy would easily destroy us because we have been made subjects of the spirit of fear. Reflecting back upon Proverbs 28:1, why does it say the righteous are as bold as a lion? Because the Spirit of Christ reigns inside them and where Jesus is, His love should abound.

Why should you be bold? Because God has not given you the spirit of fear but of power, love, and a sound mind. Why? Simply because you walk in love.

> *There is no fear in love; but perfect love casteth*
> *out fear: because fear hath torment. He that*

feareth is not made perfect in love (1 John 4:18 KJV).

Our goal as children of God is to be perfected in receiving and displaying the love of God. When I was in bondage to the spirit of fear, God gave me a revelation. I stumbled upon this Scripture in First John and He said to me, "I want you to begin to pray that My love is perfected in you." As I started praying that prayer, I began to gain dominion in areas that I did not have dominion before. I began to walk in boldness. I began to slay giants. I began to speak in public. All of the things that I was afraid of began to go away when I understood God's perfect love for me. Once He made me whole, I began to give His perfect love to others.

> *A lion, mighty among beasts, who retreats before nothing.* (Proverbs 30:30).

I want you to place yourself there for a moment. Say this aloud and let this be your declaration from today forward: "I am a lion/lioness, mighty among beasts and I retreat before nothing!"

We must ask God to give us the spirit of boldness to pursue the plans that He has established for us to fulfill. Boldness will manifest when we take upon ourselves courage in a greater measure.

WE NEVER FEAR BECAUSE GOD IS WITH US.

This courage, this love, this boldness will begin to dispel the darkness that comes against you. Children of God, we are fearless. We are confident. We are bold. We retreat before nothing. We never fear because God is with us. When we walk in confidence, we walk in freedom. And where there is freedom, there is no fear. If fear is operating in your life, you are in bondage. But God sent this book to break you free from the chains of the spirit of fear. The torment that has been plaguing you, the repeated memories of past failures, and those painful events in your life that constantly resurface—let them all go. Let God free your mind today. Walk in the liberty that Christ died to give you.

I am certain that the enemy hates for us to stand flatfooted and declare that God is our Father and He will never allow us to be ashamed. He will never leave us, neither will He forsake us. Even if we made our bed in hell, He will always be there (Psalm 139:8). That's an extreme case. However, I offer that to say that God will never bring you to a place to cause you to be embarrassed. He will never bring you to a place and not allow you to recover—even if you fail, you have the opportunity to get back up and start over again.

There is no need to fear because God is with you. It's time for us to walk in authority. It is clear that God wants us to make an exchange today. We are about to unpack this system that the enemy sets up. We are also going to gain tools on how to become free, together!

> *Two are better than one; because they have a good reward for their labour. For if they fall, the one will lift up his fellow: but woe to him that is alone when he falleth; for he hath not another to help him up. Again, if two lie together, then they have heat: but how can*

129

one be warm alone? And if one prevail against him, two shall withstand him; and a threefold cord is not quickly broken (Ecclesiastes 4:9-12 KJV).

I've heard many interpretations of this Scripture and I don't believe it is limited to marriage. I believe this word displays what friendship looks like. This passage tells us that two are better than one. It begins to teach us about the reward for labor. Labor is hanging in there with one another. When you are weak, when you are being tormented, when you are fearful, there should always be someone there to encourage you, to speak the word to you, and to release faith into your life. Again, if two lie together they have heat, but how can one be warm alone? If one prevails against him, I picture him as the enemy, Scripture says two shall withstand him. If I am weak, I need someone who is strong enough to speak the Word of God to me.

As discussed previously, I had a friend, a dear friend, who was always there to lift me up whenever I found myself in the midst of a battle. Plenty of times she didn't even know she was lifting me up. Her words were like a machine gun into the enemy's camp and she never hesitated to speak the Word of God to me. She would start prophesying to me without knowing that I was in the place I was in. That's why it's important that we have good, solid, and strong friends in Christ.

Proverbs 17:17 (KJV) says: *"A friend loveth at all times, and a brother is born for adversity."* In times of adversity, we need friends who are like our brothers and sisters in Christ, friends who are willing to stand and fight for us when it seems like the world is against us. When it seems like all hell has broken loose in our lives and we feel as though we are unable to conquer the things that are coming against us, we need somebody in our corner—a true friend. So here's what I want you to do today:

1. Ask God to surround you with people who are strong in the Word and faith.

> *Finally, brothers and sisters, whatever is true, whatever is noble, whatever is right, whatever is pure, whatever is lovely, whatever is admirable—if anything is excellent or praise-worthy—think about such things* (Philippians 4:8).

2. Ask God for a revelation of His love for you.

> *For those who are led by the Spirit of God are the children of God. The Spirit you received does not make you slaves, so that you live in fear again; rather, the Spirit you received brought about your adoption to sonship. And by him we cry, "Abba, Father." The Spirit himself testifies with our spirit that we are God's children. Now if we are children, then we are heirs—heirs of God and co-heirs with Christ, if indeed we share in his sufferings in order that we may also share in his glory* (Romans 8:14-17).

We see here that Jesus begins to encourage us and remind us that He did not give us the spirit of fear. Paul is speaking, but I believe it is the voice of Jesus speaking through him. We are sons and daughters of God. We are led by the Spirit of God. He said He didn't make us slaves to fear. He is giving us the honor of being His heirs, co-heirs with Christ.

We see the remedy for the spirit of fear is the Spirit of God. Most often where there is a spirit of fear, there is an orphan heart in action. Orphan hearts either do not yet know that they are children of God or an event has made them disbelieve that they are heirs.

Through the retraining of your thoughts and asking God for the revelation of His love for you, you can defeat the spirit of fear. It says the Spirit Himself testifies and speaks to us. Ask God for a fresh filling of His Spirit. This Spirit that Romans 8 speaks about testifies to the sons and daughters of God. We need the testimony of this Spirit. We need this testimony to make us sure and certain that we are no longer slaves but we are God's children.

3. *Retrain your thoughts.*

We talked about how to retrain your thoughts extensively in an earlier chapter, so we will keep this brief. When we look at Philippians 4:8, we find some great insight into where our focus should lie. Our mind should reflect upon things noble, right, pure, lovely, excellent, and praiseworthy. How do we get to this point where we exchange all of the negative thoughts and fill our minds with righteous thoughts? We do this in times of prayer. We do this in times of study. And we do this even with the things that we speak out of our mouths.

The Scripture says that faith comes by hearing (see Romans 10:17). So sometimes our faith is built, or broken, by the things we speak out of our mouths. The same is true for fear. When I was bound to fear, I would constantly make statements like, "I'm so afraid," "I don't sleep in the dark," "I don't do this or that." I didn't realize that every confining word that I uttered out of my mouth left a gaping hole in my faith.

Psychologists say that it takes ten truths to dispel one lie. We have to dispel the lies that the spirit of fear has fed us with the truth of God. It takes consistency. It takes persistence. It takes the Word of God. Without it, you will not defeat the spirit of fear. Keep Philippians 4:8 close to you at all times.

Please know I have faith in you! I know you can do it.

4. Retrain your speech.

> *A man's stomach shall be satisfied from the fruit of his mouth; from the produce of his lips he shall be filled. Death and life are in the power of the tongue, and those who love it will eat its fruit* (Proverbs 18:20-21 NKJV).

Just like retraining our thoughts needs to be an absolute priority, retraining our speech is just as imperative. What you say out of your mouth produces fruit—the fruit of life or the fruit of death. You make the determination. The enemy loves to use our words against us. I want you to ask God to teach you how to control your speech through the power of the Holy Spirit, and He will do that for you. The Holy Spirit is a trainer. He will teach you and train you on how to walk with God and how to manifest the fruit of your life in your life.

Psalm 141:3 (NKJV) says, *"Set a guard, O Lord, over my mouth; keep watch over the door of my lips."* This is such a great Scripture! It displays absolute dependence upon God. God can bring you gentle reminders as it relates to the things that come out of your mouth. Have you ever felt yourself in a conversation and find that you're speaking negatively about a situation or a person and the Holy Spirit begins to nudge you? That's a guard that God has set over your mouth so that you will not be led into evil. That guard is a defense, and it will keep you from speaking things that the enemy has a legal right to use against you. So when you make statements like, "I'm so afraid." Or, "I'm so this" and "I'm so that," he has a right to operate in that manner in your life.

Today I want you to ask God to set a guard over your lips. Proverbs 13:3 (NKJV) says, *"He who guards his mouth preserves his life, but he who opens wide his lips shall have destruction."* This shows us that it is partly our responsibility to watch what we say. You are a child of God. I want you to begin to think from an offensive position. You are no longer a victim; you are dangerous. Take your sword in your hand and let's get ready to cut off the head of this giant called fear!

As an emerging apostolic voice, the Kingdom of God is established within us. As apostolic men and women, we must move in extreme faith. We have the right to walk in liberty and have been given all of the necessary tools to do so. Remember—*whom the Son has made free is free indeed* (see John 8:36). So when the enemy fights against you, don't you dare retreat. Don't you dare shrink back. You must fight.

There is a terror that comes from the eyes of a lion that will cause its enemies to run. The devil wants to take over, but we have come to the place where we refuse to be taken over. We are standing in our apostolic authority.

Jesus delegated authority to you, and it's time for you to rise up and use it in His name! You must exercise your authority, or the devil will wreak havoc in your life and he will run your life. He will run your thoughts. He will train your speech. It's time for you to take your power back as a child of God. God loves you—that is reason enough for the devil to hate you! The devil would love to destroy the very intentions God has for your life; and well, he can do that through the vehicle of fear.

We are untangling you today and we are serving the devil notice that he no longer has dominion because Jesus gave you authority! You don't have to be afraid of the enemy. Jesus defeated every enemy. Jesus turned authority over to you and said that you would do more than He has ever done (see John 14:12-14). You are a child of God!

Matthew 28:18-19 says:

> *Then Jesus came to them and said, "All author-*
> *ity in heaven and on earth has been given to*
> *me. Therefore go and make disciples of all*
> *nations, baptizing them in the name of the*
> *Father and of the Son and of the Holy Spirit.*

This is where Jesus describes the assignmentof every believer. You should be readying yourself to do this. It's time for you to cast out devils. It's time for you to heal the sick. It's time for God to send you into nations. It's time for you to be a representation of Christ. We have nations to win. No fear, but all God. It's time for you to walk in apostolic authority.

Let's look at more Scripture to remind us of who we are:

Philippians 2:10 says, *"That at the name of Jesus every knee should bow, in heaven and on earth and under the earth."* Notice that every knee will bow at the name of Jesus, not a person. As true believers in Jesus Christ, we are members of His body and we are joint heirs of His authority. You are a joint heir with Christ. Take upon yourself your authority and use it for the glory of God.

Luke 10:19 says, *"I have given you authority to trample on serpents and scorpions and to overcome all the power of the enemy; nothing will harm you."* Most often our fears take advantage of us because we don't understand this Scripture. The most impactful part of this scripture is "nothing will harm you." Isn't that amazing? It says nothing. This is the promise that Jesus Christ has given us and this is what the enemy does not want you to know. Nothing by any means will hurt you. He says He's given you authority, power, over the enemy.

Retrain your thoughts. Retrain your speech and let's get ready to rumble. You are the Father's beloved. You have been bought with a price. You are no longer an orphan, but you are a son or daughter of God. It's time for you to fully embrace God's amazing plans for your life. It's time for you to understand that God has not given you the spirit of fear, but He gives you power, love, and a sound mind.

When we think about those three things, we also know that they represent a threefold cord that cannot easily be broken. When we walk in power, when we walk in love, and when we walk with sound minds, the enemy understands that we walk in God's authority. It's time for us to begin to rattle, to begin to rumble, and to begin to roll against the enemy and not shrink back. It's time for us to go forward in the name of the Lord.

PRAYER AND CONFESSION

Pray this prayer out loud:

> *Lord, I come to You, repenting for allowing the spirit of fear to operate in my life. Thank You for forgiveness. God, You have not given me the spirit of fear but of power, of love, and of a sound mind according to Second Timothy 1:7. Because of that, I'm entitled to freedom. I claim my freedom today. Holy Spirit, I pray that You would go into those areas of my mind that may have experienced a traumatic event and I pray that You would burn with the fire of the Holy Spirit every ungodly memory that has been etched in my heart and in my mind, in the name of Jesus.*
>
> *I declare that I am free. Holy Spirit, uproot every lie that has made me vulnerable and disconnected me from the voice of God. Now, Father, I pray that You would disconnect me from those voices in the name of Jesus. I pray now, God, that You would connect me to Your voice and Your voice alone. Open up a pure stream, in the name of Jesus. Father, I am thankful that You are my God and I let go of every ungodly defense, and I release myself to be vulnerable again only to You, God.*

I pray that in the name of Jesus that You would teach me how to correct my response and lead me on the pathway to pure love, which rebukes fear. Spirit of fear, you are no longer welcome here and I command you to leave me now, in the name of Jesus.

According to Proverbs 28:1, the righteous are as bold as a lion, and I take upon myself boldness. I take upon myself courage. I take upon myself apostolic authority, and I rise up with the Spirit of the Lion of the tribe of Judah operating inside me. God, I ask You for a fresh filling of Your Holy Spirit. Endow me with fresh fire from on high that I may walk in the power that You've ordained for me to walk in, in the name of Jesus.

I thank You that You give me the ability and power over my tongue that I would never speak a thing that does not bring You glory. I pray, God, and I thank You that You have given me power over my mind, that I would not think more of things that are ungodly than I do of what are pure and noble, in the name of Jesus.

I thank You, God, that in this season I'm attracting friends from the North, South, East, and West. You're giving me godly friends; and in the name of Jesus, I thank You. I'm not afraid of these relationships. I open myself now to receive godly friends. I thank God that You would heal my orphan heart. I thank You, God, that You are clearing out the clutter in my mind. In Jesus' name, I take upon myself the mind of Christ. I pray now that You would do an exchange in the Holy Spirit. God, let this carnal mind be far from me now, in the name of Jesus. Let the mind of Christ come now in the name of Jesus.

Jesus, I walk with You. Jesus, I thank You that you have given me this authority. Forgive me for not walking in it sooner. Now you have labeled me as Your son or daughter and I take upon myself every weapon that You have given me to walk in freedom, in the name of Jesus. I thank You, God, for Your love toward me, Your kindness and Your mercy, amen!

Now, walk in courage, walk in boldness, walk in the totality of all God called you to be—free from fear!

CHAPTER 11

THE SPIRIT OF WITCHCRAFT

I N THIS CHAPTER WE WILL UNCOVER THE SPIRITS OF witchcraft, divination, manipulation, control, rejection.

I was newly saved, baptized in the Holy Spirit, and in an adamant pursuit of a Spirit-filled church. I was determined and unwilling to stop until I found a place where I could experience Him. I was not yet completely healed or whole, so as a grown woman, I still craved the nurturing I never received from my mother and the affirmation and protection I missed from my father as a child, so you can imagine that my fears and abandonment wounds still ran pretty deep.

Being driven by these broken places within me, I desired to find my spiritual covering and safety.

Soon, I met a woman who seemed to understand me and all of my spiritual needs, and I didn't think twice about following her. In no time, she became my pastor. She called me her daughter. She cared for me and nurtured me. She treated me as if I were her blood, her own child. I served the church diligently. I waxed strong until the day that everything changed.

Second Samuel 3:1 (NKJV) says, *"Now there was long war between the house of Saul and the house of David. But David grew stronger and stronger, and the house of Saul grew weaker and weaker."* I remember the first time I told my pastor that I wanted to attend Bible college. I was so excited and I fully expected her to share in my excitement and be thrilled for me. Instead, I received the opposite response. She told me that all of "that education" would ruin me. She hadn't gone to theology school because the Holy Spirit was her teacher (famous line of those in rebellion to authority).

My spirit was crushed. As if our personal conversation wasn't enough, she decided to mock me at the next service. Under the guise of delivering a message for the masses, she aimed her dart directly at me and preached about people who believed they were "all that" because they were enrolling in school and how school would make "those people" (also known as me) walk away from the truth. Under her spell, that I was slowly coming out of, the other members shouted, "Amen, Pastor!" from the pews.

I was so broken and hurt because I honestly loved and adored my pastor. I was confused. I couldn't understand how or why someone who was supposed to love me could treat me this way, especially as a woman of God and beyond that, a leader. Those old familiar feelings of abandonment began to resurface once again. I even questioned myself and what I'd done to cause this. I revered this woman. In my mind, she would never hurt me, so of course it had to be something that I'd done.

UNGODLY MANIPULATION AND CONTROL

Before long though, as I spent time in prayer, I discovered that her behavior was a form of manipulation and control. She sought to keep me limited and bound to both her, her leadership, and her church. The first time a prophet ever spoke to me about my call, my pastor became very upset. I was so excited to share the word with her, but when I did, she was noticeably angry. When I would minister, she'd become agitated. Instead of loving on me and supporting me when I did well, she would admonish me and find ways to tear me down. She would ask questions like, "Why didn't that happen when I got up?"

What, other than the spirit of jealousy, would produce emotions and questions like that? But because I wasn't completely delivered from my childhood abandonment issues, I ignored every sign. My spiritual growth was stifled under her and so was every other aspect of my life. I was so devoted to her leadership and my supporting role in the church that my marriage almost failed. My children and my finances also suffered greatly, all as a result of serving under a very controlling leader. It was clear that she was threatened by me and God's vision for my life. Because I wasn't healed from my inner wounds, childhood traumas and abandonment issues, I found myself trapped in a house under a leader who refused to accept my calling because of her personal insecurities.

I decided that the best thing I could do for myself was to walk away from that place and it wasn't long before I did. I'd reached my end and I just wanted to leave peacefully. Despite how much she'd hurt me, I still wanted nothing more than to depart respectfully and honorably, hoping that she would respond in the same way. I was wrong! The ugly words that spewed from her mouth shocked me. She went as far as to try to curse me, telling me that my life and ministry were over and I was only anointed because of her. She told me that I would never go anywhere outside of her because she didn't release me! Her offensive, ungodly behavior didn't stop there. She went to all of my close friends—most of whom had joined the church after I'd invited them—and convinced them to stop speaking to me as a method of control.

Once again, I was devastated. I hadn't bashed her, gossiped about her or the church, or uttered so much as an unkind word to anyone about her. I just wanted freedom, but she made me seem like a threat and lied about me. She turned all of my friends' hearts against me and slandered my name.

Listen, people have charged me falsely and drew conclusions about me without hearing "my side." But what I have learned is that when the Holy Spirit speaks, it's best that you do what He says because it's your "next" that's on the line. My side did not matter because it is God who justifies. I was deeply wounded and my development as a daughter of God was at stake. When I escaped, I didn't look back. Eventually, I went to school against my former pastor's will and was stretched beyond measure! I found that I was more in love with God than ever!

USE YOUR MIND AND BREAK FREE

After a while, I met a woman who prayed me through to breakthrough and I am forever grateful and today, I am so blessed to see how my relationship with Him has grown immeasurably since these experiences. The Finisher speaks to me and for me because He is determined to complete what He begun.

I encountered my former pastor a few years ago, after fifteen years of no interaction with her. We had to work together for a funeral and it wasn't long before I realized that she had not changed. She attacked me almost immediately, starting by making it clear that she had the right to tell me what to do because she was, as she called herself, the "Apostle of the city." I respectfully informed her that I was not the same woman who submitted to her control—I had been delivered.

She became furious and asked me why I was acting that way. She went on to say I was treating her terribly. And then, true to character, she retaliated by releasing a word curse. She told me that she saw a heart attack coming in my future! That was enough. Jezebel's web (yes, you can find Jezebels in the pulpit too!) had been released and I did not stand passively. I rose up in authority like the empowered daughter God has shaped me to be and I *respectfully* put her in her place.

If you are ever in a similar situation, please do the same. Here's why—a pastor's release is not required in order for you to walk away from control. Church protocol means absolutely nothing when it isn't governed by God. There was a woman who was anointed to break curses and she prayed for me; I will never forget her. I walk in freedom from word curses today and you can too!

> ## CHURCH PROTOCOL MEANS ABSOLUTELY NOTHING WHEN IT ISN'T GOVERNED BY GOD.

If your leaders are known for cursing people for leaving their church, that's called witchcraft, I admonish you to get out of there! You do not have to submit to witchcraft in the name of submission. You never have to listen to threats or accept any word curses over your life. You serve the God of angel armies and there is a whole team of angels fighting for you! Your life is not over after these types of experiences. It's just begun! The type of bondage that I experienced and that you may have also encountered can cause you to disobey God to please people. The fear of people brings a snare (see Proverbs 29:25). You must gain the courage to walk away! If you have left a house like this, your first step should be to seek deliverance. Deliverers should be delivered first!

SPIRIT OF REJECTION

Years after my experience, I started pastoring; I remember suffering greatly from the spirit of rejection because I had not yet discovered my deliverer. Every pastor needs deliverance! Rejection in a senior leader is horrible; but sadly, it's an epidemic in today's churches. Rejected leaders have an unhealthy view. They see others as a threat and it shows up whenever someone attempts to challenge authority or even innocently do something outside of their control. The spirits of suspicion and paranoia rule in their minds and therefore they are always waiting for the next person to hurt them. If you do not seek deliverance from your rejection, it will cause you to operate as a victim. In turn, you will transfer that spirit to those who have decided to partner with you, leading them to believe that you have been victimized by those who "left you."

Members come and go, and as a leader, not only should you not be offended, but you should also not allow those negative feelings to permeate your church. If you're under this type of leader, repent for allowing another person to control you. You were bought and persuaded. As a son or daughter of God, your allegiance is to Him first and you must be delivered from man-pleasing and ministry idolatry. No human being should have the power to control you.

Sometimes pastors are controlling because they are afraid of people leaving their church. It's a fear that many new pastors face and must overcome, but I know many who never do. When someone leaves their church, they throw themselves a huge pity party. This is one thing that I had to learn as a senior pastor—people are not mine, they belong to God. I don't want to force anyone to stay in my church and you shouldn't either. The problem for some pastors is that they were seduced into a church, promised a position, and now they're in prison. This is why it is essential for leaders to go through deliverance before trying to lead anyone. If you are a pastor or in a leadership position and haven't been delivered, it's not too late. Locate your deliverers! Jesus came to set the captives free!

The types of control commonly found in the church and among church leadership can come in many forms. Some examples include:

- Regulates your paycheck

- Tells you how to spend your money

- Releases word curses against you when you don't obey; curses such as death, anointing or ministry will dry up, and even death

- Tells you how to manage your home

- Demands to have priority above your spouse

- Taunts you for attending ministry school out of fear

There are some instances in which input from leadership about your personal affairs is warranted. If you are in a leadership position, a leader has a right to ask how you manage your home and offer strategies about improvements. Your leader should have conversations with you about debt management and provide teaching about walking in integrity in every area of your life.

However, there are extremes to what we call control. What I am talking about is a church taking your money, asking for W2s to prove that you're tithing correctly, paying your bills with your paycheck, keeping the change, and dictating your every move without allowing you to make your own decisions. You are *not* a robot—you are a human being with a will that God has granted to all of humankind. Colossians 2:18 states:

> *Do not let anyone who delights in false humility and the worship of angels disqualify you. Such a person also goes into great detail about what they have seen; they are puffed up with idle notions by their unspiritual mind.*

I know that while your spirit is telling you to break free, you believe that you should be loyal to your leaders and your church. My apostle, Dr. Matthew Stevenson, taught me that there is a perverted type of loyalty called "Lethal Loyalty." Some of us are serving Ahabs in the name of being loyal. You will not receive rewards for this. Don't even think about it. This is not humility and it's not honor. It's enabling control. It gives demons access and power over you. Repent and break free from control!

JEZEBEL SPIRIT

So let's talk about this Jezebelic spirit operating in the church, especially in leadership. I shared with you my experience with a previous pastor who I would undoubtedly put in this category. Characteristically, Jezebels are controlling, insecure, and manipulative spirits disguised as prophets. While Jezebel appears to be a powerful leader, beneath the allure, grandeur, and seduction, their teaching is misleading and not of God. Revelation 2:20 says:

*Nevertheless, I have this against you: You
tolerate that woman Jezebel, who calls herself
a prophet. By her teaching she misleads my
servants into sexual immorality and the eating
of food sacrificed to idols.*

Jezebelic leaders use coercion and seduction to keep
their members bound to their church and it has to stop. Pastors like these seduce people into their church and then
they use forms of control and manipulation to keep them!
They will say things such as, "All I have is you. If you leave, I
will be all alone." They whine, cry, and will even show up at
events that you are attending to ensure they "keep an eye on
you." If you find yourself in this type of situation, repent and
free yourself.

The insecure nature of the spirit of Jezebel often man-
ifests as control. Jezebelic leaders typically discourage
their members from learning from other ministries or leaders. They will even go as far as to directly forbid members
from attending other conferences and trainings due to their
own insecurities.

If your leadership cannot provide what you need to grow
in Christ but insists on hindering you from finding what you
need outside of their church, they are nobody's leader. They
are witches in clergy robes. God doesn't control us and no
one else should either. Granted, if you are a pastor, you must
protect your flock. There are some churches that your members should not attend due to bad doctrine, seducing spirits,
and other activities that are not of God. And yes, there are likely
bad trainers in the world too. But everyone is not a threat, so
we cannot always hide behind this excuse.

Raise people up in truth so they can for themselves righteously discern the truth from a lie! If your pastor (or you) started doing this because you were afraid that people would walk away or you are afraid of failing, know that there is deliverance and freedom for you. I'll be as frank about this topic as I possibly can—these types of leaders need to have a seat until they receive deliverance. If your leader or leaders are insecure, stop and pray for them right now. Your next step will be to leave that church behind and seek a spiritual house that can provide training and development.

A controlling leader is driven by fear and will never make your development a priority. The reality is that you will never grow in a church under this type of leadership, so it's okay to walk away. As an emerging apostolic voice, godly leadership is so critical for you. Your leader has been crafted to cover you in times of adversity and their mantle was designed with you in mind!

You need to grow into a strong individual in a strong house or a house that's developing strongly. It doesn't have to be the perfect house—it just has to be the right house for you! It's important to be part of the right house because your process is tied to that house! There is a leader and there are people who are assigned to process you. The process and protocols of that house will sharpen you and make you ready for your assignment. Do not reject the process.

Connecting to the right leader changed my life and I know it will do the same for you. Seek God and pray diligently for your destined leader.

If you've ever been part of any of the things I have described, please know that you have been called to bring deliverance to a generation that has been abused by many. Find your house, be delivered, and tell your story!

Calling all sons and daughters! Calling all deliverers! Calling truth bearers, righteous and fearless ones, those who bear the mark of Jesus Christ, and those who have the heart of Christ! Rise up deliverers! I am calling you. Your destined leaders are calling you. Those who you were born to lead are calling you. God is calling you!

PRAYER AND CONFESSION

Father, in the name of Jesus, You are holy. There is no one greater than You and no one who can compare to You. According to Genesis 1, You have created me in Your image and after Your likeness. Thank You. I am stepping into a new day and I receive fresh revelations and insight concerning my destiny, in Jesus' name. I break all generational curses of pride, rebellion, witchcraft, idolatry, death, destruction, failure, sickness, infirmity, fear, schizophrenia, and rejection, in the name of Jesus.

I take authority over all wickedness and release myself from all control and fear of people. I break Jezebel's spell and cut the cords connected to the spirit of Ahab, in the name of Jesus. I declare a new day has dawned! Lord Jesus, I invite You to be Lord of my mind, emotions, decisions, feelings, and relationships again. Protect me from the influences of those who would take advantage of me. I want to be led by You and Your God-given authority. I thank You for all that You have done and will do now and in my future. I reject the effects of the spirit of abandonment and receive the Spirit of God as His child, in Jesus' name.

CHAPTER 12

STRATEGIES IN
WARFARE

YOU ARE A CHILD OF GOD AND YOU HAVE BEEN ARMED
with weapons—your word, your worship, and your
prayer. It's time to wage war. Your weapons are aids at times
of attack and battle against the kingdom of darkness. These
are functional weapons, which mean they work all the time
and they are to be used offensively and defensively. These
weapons have been proven and tested over time and they
cannot fail. Why? Because the Word of God says so!

A weapon is designed or used for inflicting bodily
harm or physical damage. A weapon of mass destruction
is a chemical, biological, or radioactive defense, capable of

causing widespread death and destruction. As His sons and daughters, God wants you to become accustomed to and acquainted with the use of your weapons.

Let's look at each of them more closely.

1. HOW ARE PRAYERS USED AS A WEAPON?

According to Ephesians 6:18-19 (NKJV), prayer is used as a weapon to bring all matters into alignment:

> ***Praying always*** *with all prayer and supplication in the Spirit, being watchful to this end with all perseverance and supplication for all the saints—and for me, that utterance may be given to me, that I may open my mouth boldly to make known the mystery of the gospel.*

Isn't that powerful? He said to pray always—with what? *"Prayer and supplication in the spirit!"* He admonishes them to do this *always* because this is a secret weapon that cannot be easily intercepted by demonic spirits. We should look at prayer and intercession as a lifetime career, not something you can quit. *Praying always* is not something that you can take rest from. The kingdom of darkness is always trying to advance against you. Because of that, you must pray. *Always!*

C. S. Lewis wrote in his book *Mere Christianity*, "This world is an enemy occupied territory and that Christianity is the story of how a rightful king has landed. That king is Jesus, and He's calling us all to take part of this great campaign of sabotage." What exactly are we sabotaging? We are sabotaging the kingdom of darkness. The enemy put a plan in place to advance, conquer, and overthrow the plan of God. Believers know that the Word of God stands and God cannot lie.

Prayer is how we spiritually fight back against the enemy. Prayer is fundamental and it is a weapon of war. It is a vehicle, a powerful tool that God gives us as believers. Prayer gives us the ability to fight against the enemy and win. When God tells us to pray in the Spirit, He does so because the enemy cannot interpret what you are saying in the Spirit. When you are coached to pray in the Spirit, this is not something you are doing for your leader—it is for you. God wants to fortify you so that the enemy cannot intercept or overthrow the plan, thing, or person you are bringing before God.

God is looking for those who are willing to learn what the weapon of prayer should be used for and use it. When we pray in the Spirit, those prayers cannot be constricted by natural barriers such as the English language and limited vocabulary. When we pray in the natural, our prayers can be restricted and intercepted. Someone can hear you and pray a prayer that is contrary or to oppose it. However, when you pray in the Spirit, it's a private conversation between you and God that cannot be interfered with. It's a conversation that can penetrate. It can go through realms. It can move from this place to the second heaven and all the way to the third heaven.

Those who move and pray have the ability to touch the heavens and the ears of God. Your prayers are powerful weapons that cannot be restricted when you pray in the Spirit. The enemy will fight you, but God is greater than the enemy that comes against you. All God is looking for is a group of believers who will use the weapon of prayer. Are you willing to use the weapon of prayer?

We are on a battlefield; this is not a place to rest, it is not a place to sit. When you are in the midst of war, there is an opponent and there is you. Your opponent wants to destroy you. This is the time for you to rise and use your weapons against the kingdom of darkness. The battlefield represents a particular place for a specified season or an appointment for war that we will all come to. There are appointments for war, yet many Christians don't believe that. Every war is not initiated by hell. Some wars are initiated by God. Warfare will come until whatever it is that God intends for us to get is obtained. Do you know that if God intends for you to get something, you have to war for it? There are some things that will come to you with ease and there are some things you have to go to war for.

It's time for you to war!

Your opponent has one goal in mind—to destroy. That's why in times of warfare, you can't afford to be isolated. You need to be connected with those of like kind. You need to be in the presence of God. Acts 3:19 (NKJV) says, *"times of refreshing may come from the presence of the Lord."* It is the presence of God that will refresh you. First Corinthians 12:12 (KJV) says, *"For as the body is one, and hath many members, and all the members of that one body, being many, are one body: so also is Christ."* When you come together for prayer, it is God's intention that you tap into that corporate anointing. That corporate anointing will cause the presence of God to be released in a way that you cannot experience when praying alone in your car or your bedroom.

Man or woman of God, I'm coming against the part of you that goes into isolation every time you find yourself in a place of war. As people of prayer and intercession, our most potent weapon is to have a clear understanding of how the enemy operates. Satan is legalistic and he never plays fair. We see this in the case of Job. In Job 1, there was a conversation between Satan and God. They were negotiating about Job. Job was favored by God and was a wealthy man. He had an abundance of things and had a great family. All of a sudden God gives Satan permission to touch Job. He removed the hedge of protection around Job.

Do you know that there are times in your life when you've been *"considered"* by God? (See Job 1:8; 2:3 KJV.) This doesn't happen because God is displeased with you. It happens when He has faith in you. God never brought you to a place of war and intended you to lose. He always intends you to win. It is your responsibility to rise up and win. You have to use your weapons. You will have to rely on your weapon of prayer to handle the delay that is inevitable. Sometimes in warfare, we are confused and feel like God is not answering us. Instead of holding fast, we give up, drop all of our weapons, and surrender to the enemy. You cannot give it all over to Satan and his army that easily. You cannot surrender to your enemy. It's time for you to go back into the fight.

The book of Daniel teaches us how to deal with the wait while we're in warfare. Daniel had a humble heart and was in right standing with God. He was also a man of prayer. In Daniel 10:12, the angel Gabriel told Daniel, *"Do not be afraid, Daniel. Since the first day that you set your mind to gain understanding and to humble yourself before your God, your words were heard, and I have come in response to them."*

God will come in response to your prayer. Sometimes, you have to keep worshiping your way through it. Sometimes, you have to keep praying your way through it. Sometimes you have to have a conversation with God. Cry out to Him and say, "God, if You could just talk to me for a moment. I know Your Word says that You hear me when I pray. Please explain to me what this delay is." He is your Father. Ask Him. He will answer.

Daniel prayed and Gabriel came with an explanation. Like Daniel's, some of your prayers are being restricted in the second heaven. I'm here to tell you that it's not your job to deal with what's happening in the second heaven—that is the angels' job. Gabriel fought that battle. You may be talking about binding in the second heaven, but God never called you to bind anything there. Learn how to use your help, the angelic host, an entire company of angels assigned to assist you, so you can see your breakthrough. Breakthrough is coming!

When you are a person of prayer, the Breaker will go before you. Who is the Breaker? His name is Jesus. He is Jehovah Gabor, the God who battles. He's the God who fights for us. The Breaker will go before you. God will run interference for us. He is the God who will deal with our delay. He's the God who deals with what fights against us. Micah 2:13 calls Him the Lord of the **Breakthrough**. In First Corinthians 3:7 we learn Him to be the God who brings the **Increase**. In First Peter 5:10, He is called the God of all **Grace**. You see, He's the God of the B.I.G. and He has B.I.G. designed and prepared just for you, believe it!

Proper Discernment

Proper discernment is necessary in times of battle. It is important that you ask God to show you the source of your attack. You need to know what weapon to pull out for what type of demon spirit you are up against. You also need to know if the war you are fighting is internal or external. If God has sent something or someone to you to deal with your character or your heart, it may seem like war but it's really the hand of God seeking to purge you. He wants to pull everything that is working against you out of you. So, sometimes, you're fighting a war with yourself. It's pertinent that you know the source of your attack.

Jesus understood the source of the pressure that He was experiencing. In Matthew 26:36-46, He was dealing with the most challenging situation in His life. If it were us in the garden, we would have fought Judas. If it were us in the garden, we would have attacked every soldier who was coming to threaten our lives. But God shows us that there are times when we should not attack the soldier, but submit to the death. Since Jesus understood the source of the attack, at that moment, He submitted to the death that was to come. He let the soldiers lead Him to slaughter because He understood His purpose was to be the Lamb of God. When you understand your purpose and when you understand the source of your attack, you will gladly go to the place of slaughter.

You may be fighting while God is trying to destroy those enemies that are working in you. You may be fighting while God is trying to use this warfare as a platform to your next place. Sometimes the war is purposed to bring you into your new place. It's designed to bring you into a fresh place, child of God. You've got to understand that the weapons of your warfare are not carnal—they are mighty spiritual weapons from God to pull down strongholds (2 Corinthians 10:4).

When you understand, as a child of God, that your weapons make you mighty and dangerous against the kingdom of darkness, you understand you don't have to break a sweat. All you have to do is bide your time and wait your turn. You are coming out of this and you're coming out on top. Your weapon is your prayer.

Satan will strategize and look for great opportunities to slow you down. He wants to destroy your effectiveness. He wants to eventually attack you in such a way that you will never recover. He wants to see all the breath leave out of you. But I'm here to let you know that as long as you have breath in your body, there is always opportunity to recover. There is always an opportunity to cross over and make it to the other side. That moment when you think you are about to die, the Holy Spirit will come and resuscitate you and breathe life back into you again.

I am a living witness. God is a good, good God. He will never leave us at the place of war. He comes to bring us out. That's why Acts 3:20 says we need a time of refreshing. God will never leave you in war long enough for you to die. He leaves you in the war long enough for you come out with the goods.

You may have aborted or walked away from the war instead of toward it. You may have missed your season of training, but God needs to teach your hands to war and your fingers to fight. He's going to do that on the battlefield. This is a career. You can't quit. You can't stop battling. You are an emerging, apostolic vessel—one who has been graced for such a time as this. You have the mantle to fight against darkness. God has equipped and prepared you for this time.

2. HOW IS MY WORD USED AS A WEAPON?

We're going to talk about the Word of God and the word of our testimony. The word is a weapon; Second Corinthians 10:3-6 (KJV) says:

> *For though we walk in the flesh, we do not war after the flesh: (For the weapons of our warfare are not carnal, but mighty through God to the pulling down of strong holds;) Casting down imaginations, and every high thing that exalteth itself against the knowledge of God, and bringing into captivity every thought to the obedience of Christ; and having in a readiness to revenge all disobedience, when your obedience is fulfilled.*

In spiritual warfare, we have multiple weapons. We have the weapon of faith. We have the weapon of the name of Jesus. We have the weapon of the blood of Jesus. We have the weapon of praise. But I want to talk about the weapon of the Word, which is the sword of the spirit and the weapon of our testimony. God wants us to understand the power of the sword of the Spirit. Ephesians 6:16-17 (KJV):

> *Above all, taking the shield of faith, wherewith ye shall be able to quench all the fiery darts of*

*the wicked. And take the helmet of salvation,
and the sword of the Spirit, which is the word
of God.*

The Romans used a short double-edged sword called a gladius. These weapons are small and light enough for a soldier to carry for long distances. It was easier to handle and to maneuver in battle. While a shield, helmet, and breastplate were used only for defense purposes, a sword was used for both offense and defense. For defense, the soldier used the sword to deflect the enemy's blows. As an offensive weapon, the sword was used to attack the enemy until the weapon seriously injured or killed the assailant.

When we think about the Word of God, we usually think about it in the context of offense. But when we are in battle, it is our responsibility to wield our sword in defense as well. This is why we have to know the Word. When we are in battle, the first thing to go is usually our attention span. We can't sit down long enough to read God's Word, the Bible. Why? Because the lack of focus is a weapon of war that the enemy uses against us. The enemy will release that weapon of war against our mind. He understands that when we get in God's Word, those ties that he has around our mind will begin to pop.

The Word of God is the power of God unto salvation. It is the Word of God, the sword of the Spirit, which has that double edge. It pierces and divides the soul asunder. The Word of God has the power to be used as a blow against the enemy when we are under attack. When we understand that we are sons and daughters, we also understand that war is inevitable. We use our sword of the Spirit as a defensive weapon before we find ourselves on the battlefield. It is our responsibility to read the Word, to know the Word, and to speak the Word. It is a weapon that is released in the atmosphere that can be used ahead of time. That Word will begin to take form. It will begin to take shape in the atmosphere. It begins to create. When you release it, it does what it is intended to do. God is not a man that He should lie, neither is He the son of man that He should repent (Numbers 23:19). If He spoke it, it shall surely come to pass. When you speak it according to His Word, it is as good as God speaking it. His Word has weight, authority, and power so when you release the Word, it rises above everything in your life and it begins to create.

The Word is a weapon against Satan. When he attacks your mind, we think about Second Corinthians 10:4 (NKJV), *"For the weapons of our warfare are not carnal but mighty in God for pulling down strongholds."* What is this Scripture referring to? It is talking about a stronghold that has been formed in your mind. The Word of God is to be used against strongholds that are formed in your mind. You have the power through the Word of God to cast down ungodly imaginations. Whenever an imagination forms, it forms and then it creates. An imagination can create a lie so powerful that it can make you see a situation as true when it's really a lie. It's only the truth, the sword of the Spirit that has the power to undo everything that the lie has done.

Satan understands where we are weak and, in war, he always plays on our weaknesses. When God tells you to fast when you're in a war, what would Satan want you to do? Eat. He understands that if you are a slave to your belly and you like to eat, he can distract you, weaken you, and ultimately destroy by causing those cravings to intensify—if you let him.

When I am fasting, I am always overwhelmed with the smell of bacon. Satan knows that it's one of my weaknesses. My senses increase. I can smell fried chicken from four miles away. He understands that if he can get me to eat, he can strip me of the power that God wants to release to me as the result of the fast. Fasting has the power to release the bands of wickedness. Fasting has the power to break those bands. Satan knows this so he will use everything he can to break you.

If he knows that you love sleep, Satan will use that desire for rest against you, too. Some people love to sleep—even beyond normal. We can't produce anything because we sleep away every free moment we have. Some sleep is due to health issues but some is just demonic. If your eyes get heavy every time you open the Word or a book to learn something, that's warfare and witchcraft. The enemy knows there is something on those pages that will empower you to change, to grow, and to be strengthened, edified, and ready for war. He fears that you are going to be empowered to do more than you've ever done. That you're going to be empowered in your purpose and understand it very quickly. This is why he uses our weaknesses against us. He wants us to yield to temptation and forfeit our next victory.

We saw this type of attack on Jesus during His forty-day fast. Satan came to Jesus and said, *"If You are the Son of God, command that theses stones become bread"* (Matthew 4:3 NKJV). Although Jesus was and is the Son of God, at that time, He had a physical body and He was susceptible to temptation. He understands us. He is not disappointed when you are tempted; He's disappointed when you *fall* into temptation. All of us can experience cravings. All of us can go through longings. All of us can be tempted, but He's only disappointed when we fall into the temptation.

We have to take it upon ourselves to model what Jesus gave us. Jesus gave us the best example of how to deal with temptation—He responded with the Word. The Word of God does what? It searches our heart. It helps us to prepare for battle. It can enable us to discern and to detect the enemy. Sometimes we are looking for the enemy in the same place. But sometimes, he's purposely coming from another place.

That's why we are sideswiped; we have not properly discerned the whole thing, the whole battle. You're looking for Satan in the area of lust, but he's coming for you in the area of your belly. You have to understand where he's coming from. You have to be watchful and prayerful. Scripture says the adversary, the devil, roams like a roaring lion seeking whom he may devour (1 Peter 5:8). He is looking to destroy you. But you, as a son or daughter of God, have the power to rise above. The Word of God, according to Hebrews 4:12, *"is living and active. Sharper than any double-edged sword, it penetrates even to dividing soul and spirit, joints and marrow...."*

The Word judges the intentions and the attitudes of the heart. That's why you need the Word of God. You cannot afford to have your heart lie to you. Your heart is deceitful. Your heart is wicked. There is no way to discern a lie without the truth of God being alive and active in you. Your heart will betray you. Your heart will make you believe the lie is the truth; and before you know it, you are led astray. But as a child of God, you are going to stay on course.

I decree you're going to use your weapons and discern. The Word penetrates and divides. It separates the soul and the spirit. It separates our emotions from the mind, will, and plans of God. It will subdue the spirit of temptation. Jesus Himself used the Word of God to resist the temptation from Satan. He used the sword of the Spirit. He said, "It is written" every time; and when the enemy thought he could seduce Him, he lost.

As a Kingdom heir, you cannot be seduced by things. God wants to kill the parts of you that can be bought. God wants to kill the parts of you that can be seduced. He wants to kill the parts of you that can be led astray because of a gift, a microphone, and what appears to be greater. He wants to kill those parts of you because He wants to make you stable and make you more capable than you've ever been.

The Word of Our Testimony

Last, we should think of the word of our testimony. Revelation 12:11 says, *"They triumphed over him [Satan] by the **blood of the lamb and by the word of their testimony**; they did not love their lives so much as to shrink from death."* Your experiences, your testimony is the source behind everything that God will do in your life. When God brings you out of war, He gives you a testimony. When you have conquered something—anything—you have a testimony and it will be the power behind everything that God wants you to do in and for His Kingdom.

Understand me when I tell you that once you have been delivered from lust and you have been tested and proven and gone through deliverance, you are the greatest weapon. You are an arrow to be shot into the kingdom of darkness against the kingdom of lust because now you are a banner. You are a standard to say that there is victory over lust. There is victory over homosexuality. There is victory over perversion. Do you know how I did it? I did it because Jesus did it. God wants to make you a standard. He wants to give you powerful weapons. He wants to give you the weapon of the word of your testimony.

It is time to submit to being tested, to being tried, to being proven. Once you've been tested, tried, and proven, God can do anything with your life. Once you have taken the time to submit, God will shoot you out as an arrow into the earth and He will make your name great. I'm here to tell you that if you have ants in your pants, you better take the time to submit. Man of God, woman of God, you do not have time to play; your destiny is at stake. When God brings you to war, He brings you to this war to win. You are in it to win it. You will not be defeated. You will not lose; God is going to give you the victory. Greater is He who is in you than he that is in the world (1 John 4:4). Understand that God is standing up. He's ready to stand up for you and be great in your life.

The power of God is real. The power of prayer is real. The power of the Word is real, and the power of your testimony is real. God is bringing you into authenticity. He's bringing a threefold cord that shall not be easily broken in your life. God is in the business of dealing with your enemies. God is ready for you to wield your weapons and to wield your sword. He is ready for you to open your mouth, release the Word of God, and begin to declare.

As a child of God, there are people assigned to you. There are nations in your loins that are locked up and waiting for you to use the weapons that God has given you. It's time for you to use your weapons.

3. HOW DO I USE MY WORSHIP AS A WEAPON?

Second Chronicles 20:18-24 (NKJV) reads:

> And Jehoshaphat bowed his head with his face to the ground, and all Judah and the inhabitants of Jerusalem bowed before the Lord, worshiping the Lord. Then the Levites of the children of the Kohathites and of the children of the Korahites **stood up to praise the Lord God of Israel with voices loud and high.**

> So they rose early in the morning and went out into the Wilderness of Tekoa; and as they went out, Jehoshaphat stood and said, "Hear me, O Judah and you inhabitants of Jerusalem: Believe in the Lord your God, and you shall be established; believe His prophets, and you shall prosper." And when he had consulted with the people, he appointed those who should **sing to the Lord, and who should praise the beauty of holiness,** as they went out before the army and were saying: "Praise the Lord, for His mercy endures forever."

> Now when **they began to sing and to praise**, the Lord set ambushes against the people of Ammon, Moab, and Mount Seir, who had come against Judah; and they were defeated. For the people of Ammon and Moab stood up against the inhabitants of Mount Seir to utterly kill and destroy them. And when they

had made an end of the inhabitants of Seir,
they helped to destroy one another.

So when Judah came to a place overlooking
the wilderness, they looked toward the multi-
tude; and there were their dead bodies, fallen
on the earth. No one had escaped.

When we look at this story in Second Chronicles, Jehoshaphat bowed his head with his face to the ground and everyone bowed before the Lord worshiping Him. He led by example. They understood that to win this battle, they had to lead out in worship. Then they stood up to praise the Lord with their voices on high. What were they doing? They were releasing their praise on high to get the attention of heaven. They understood, with heaven, they were outnumbered. They rose early in the morning to go out and position themselves as God had commanded them. God began to instruct them. God said, "Listen, this is how you are going to win this battle."

Jehoshaphat inspired them by saying, *"Believe in the Lord your God, and you shall be established; believe His prophets, and you shall prosper."* He encouraged them to believe God. He told them to have faith, to be surrounded by people who have an ear to hear; and finally, he commanded them to believe in the prophets. Jehoshaphat added a weapon to the battle—he appointed singers unto the Lord to praise Him in the beauty of holiness. What a mighty choir this must have been.

Can you imagine this? These believers are surrounded by enemies and, all of a sudden, they stop what they're doing, undistracted by the enemy. They stop and bow to the ground, with a choir singing, listening to the prophetic voice and hearing what the Lord is saying. They went out before the army and began to sing, "Praise the Lord, for His mercy endures forever!" They understood that to win, they needed to call on God. They lifted up their voices. Worship was the only weapon they had. They didn't have anything else that would subdue that army other than worship.

Lift your voice, man of God! Lift your voice, woman of God! For His mercy endures forever. If you are in a war and find that God is not responding, lift your voice in worship. This is how we get the attention of God.

Second Chronicles 20:22 says, *"Now when they began to sing and to praise, the Lord set ambushes against the people of Ammon, Moab, and Mount Seir, who had come against Judah; and they were defeated."*

What are ambushes? God sent a force of angels that the enemy could not run or hide from. They thought that they were going to ambush God's people, but God ambushed their enemy. Do you need God to deal with your enemy? You may have been trying to fight in your own strength, but if you learn to lift your voice and worship, God will deal with your enemies. Those people who harass you, those things that are coming against you, those unseen weapons and in those spiritually high places, God will ambush your enemies.

I decree that you have testimonies that are waiting for you to walk through your war with worship. But you can't get there because you have not been able to run and hide from the weapon that has been sent against your mind. Begin to lift your voice and cry, for the Lord is good and

His mercy endures forever. Your circumstance should never dictate what your worship is. When you feel your circumstances taking over you, it's time to increase your worship. You need God to send ambushes against the enemies that have been harassing you.

If you are working in your own strength, God is going to retire you when you understand what your weapons are. You're going to begin to use your word of testimony. You're going to begin to use your prayer. You're going to begin to use your worship. You need to retire doing this in your own strength. You need to rest from striving in the flesh and pick up your spiritual weapons. The weapons of your warfare are not carnal, but mighty through God to the pulling down of strongholds. You may need to learn to plug in through worship. Plant this in your heart and declare it out loud as often as you think about it: "Outside of Him, I'm nothing. In Him, as a dangerous weapon, I am powerful because greater is God in me than the enemy in the world."

When you worship, God will destroy every enemy. You might be in a battle, but understand that God is looking for your response. What will your response be in time of battle? What are you going to do when hell comes against you? Pray this prayer, child of God:

> *I will look unto the hill from where comes my help. I will lift my voice in adoration to the great King and Lord of glory; to God Almighty, my Deliverer, and my Strength. I will lift my voice because God is for me. When God is for me, no devil in hell can be against me.*

I understand that though I may be attacked,
God fights for me. God is there for me!

The Bible says your enemies are going to fall by your side, a thousand at one side and ten thousand at the other (Psalm 91). God is in the midst of bringing you out. You need to learn how to worship your way through.

Pray in earnest:

I will lift my voice unto God my help. I will lift
my voice unto God. I might be cornered right now,
but the more I'm backed into a corner, the more
I will worship. I might be cornered right now but
I still have a voice and I will lift my voice to the
Lord and I will worship.

Are you willing to worship? Do you understand the power of worship will get the attention of heaven? God has angels upon angels ready to come and fight for you. When Jesus was on the cross, He said if He wanted to He could call 1,000 angels, a legion of angels. There is an angel army waiting to assist you, but you have to learn how to lift your voice and worship. Like He told Jehoshaphat, you have no need to fight this battle (2 Chronicles 20:17). Gather the people and worship.

All God is looking for is a group of believers willing to be brought into the place of worship and truly worship Him. God is bringing death to some of your enemies. They all lay dead. One breath of God can destroy all of your enemies at the same time. Will you worship Him? Worship will bring you into the place of victory. Worship guarantees your victory. Say, "God, make me dangerous!" What you've been doing up to this point hasn't been working, but God has given you a strategy. It's in your worship, in your prayer, and in the Word.

Again I ask, will you worship Him?

About the Author

Yolanda Stith was born in Baltimore, Maryland. She is a servant of God and has acquired much understanding in the areas of prayer and spiritual warfare. She is the definition of an overcomer. Apostle Yolanda is the President of Preparing His Bride Ministries and Pastor of ANWA— Baltimore. She earned a Bachelor's degree in Biblical Studies from Lancaster Bible College. She and her family live in Pennsylvania.

For more information about
Yolanda Stith's ministry:

phone: 410-664-0103

email: info@tolandastith.com

website: www.YolandaStith.com

social media: Facebook, instagram,
yolandastithministries